D1243042

JOHN WESLEY IN WALES

PLATE 1

JOHN WESLEY
From an engraving by Bland of a portrait by Nathaniel Hone, R.A.

JOHN WESLEY
IN WALES,
1739–1790

Entries from his Journal and Diary
relating to Wales.

Edited, with an Introduction,

by

A. H. WILLIAMS

CARDIFF
UNIVERSITY OF WALES PRESS
1971

© *University of Wales Press*, 1971

PRINTED IN GREAT BRITAIN

To the Memory of

R. T. JENKINS

C.B.E., M.A. D.LITT., LL.D.

1881–1969

PREFACE

SOME years ago, while working on the history of Welsh Wesleyan Methodism, I felt the need of a volume containing all the references to Wales which appear in John Wesley's *Journal*. In more recent years my experience as Editor of *Bathafarn*, the Journal of the Historical Society of the Methodist Church in Wales, has reinforced that earlier need and has suggested that it is shared with many others. The *Journal* runs to four volumes in the popular Everyman Edition and to eight in the Standard Edition edited by Nehemiah Curnock, but the one is now out of print and the other is over fifty years old. It occurred to me therefore that it might be useful to students of the religious history of Wales, as well as to the general reader, if all the accounts written by John Wesley of his many visits to Wales were extracted from the complete *Journal* and edited in the light of our present knowledge. Such a volume, one also felt, might serve as a source-book for teachers and for students in our Sixth Forms and colleges.

John Wesley kept a Diary from the age of 21 until a few months of his death in 1791 at the advanced age of 87. Methodically and minutely, he recorded in it how he spent his time, and with its aid he wrote the *Journal*, which now ranks with the best-known Journals and Diaries of the English language. The *Journal* was published in 21 Parts (or Extracts) over many years, and is fairly complete. But the Diary was never intended for publication, and was written in a code of Wesley's invention which baffled all attempts to break it until, one day, Nehemiah Curnock hit upon the key. He therefore published it with the Journal in his Standard Edition—or all that remains of it, for it is sad to think that so little has survived. During the years covered by these fragments, Wesley visited Wales on six occasions, and the relevant entries have been printed in italics immediately preceding the corresponding entries in the *Journal*.

As for the *Journal*, all serious students of Methodism now rely on the Standard Edition, but Curnock and his assistants (or 'experts', as he called them), though they performed a magnificent task, were no more infallible than the rest of us. Moreover, one could hardly expect them to devote detailed attention to Wales (or, for that matter, to any other part of the British Isles), for that would have increased their labours considerably and enlarged the eight volumes still further. Again, one had to be reassured that they had done full justice to the earlier, printed versions for, surprising though it may seem, not a single portion of the *Journal* covered by this volume has survived in manuscript. This could only be done by reference to the Extracts as they had appeared, and collating them with second and later editions in which Wesley (and others after him) had made some corrections. I have not hesitated to follow Curnock's annotations whenever I found myself in agreement with him (his text is well-nigh perfect), to depart from them whenever I felt they required correction, and above all to amplify them in the light of subsequent research into Methodist and Welsh history.

An explanatory word on the use of place-names is necessary. With one doubtful exception, their identification presented no difficulty, but their spelling has posed a problem. There could be no question of reproducing Wesley's brave attempts to spell them, but should they be printed uniformly in their Welsh form or in their English equivalent—Cardiff or Caerdydd, Llanfair-ym-Muallt or Builth Wells? There is much to be said for the former; there would be even more if this were a Welsh version of the *Journal*. But apart from other considerations, some Welsh place-names, one fears, would be puzzling even to Welsh ears and would leave the English reader completely confounded; not every Welshman, it is safe to say, would recognize the charming Llanfihangel Torymynydd as the more prosaic Devauden. On the other hand, there is nothing to be said for the modern, corrupt anglicized spelling of so many place-names when they are so easily recognizable in their correct Welsh dress; Llanelli, Llandeilo, and Caernarfon, to name but three, are no more difficult to identify than Llanelly, Llandilo, and Carnarvon. The difficulty has been to know where to draw the line—between Cydweli and Kidwelly for example, or Crucywel and Crickhowell. I cannot claim even to have satisfied myself by the compromise I have adopted, but I trust the forms I have used will give no cause to the monoglot English reader to throw up his arms in despair, or the ardent Welshman to clench his teeth in righteous indignation.

It is a pleasure to acknowledge the assistance I have received from several quarters. Dr. John C. Bowmer of the Methodist Archives and Research Centre, London, and the staffs of the British Museum, the National Library of Wales, Cardiff Central Library, and the Glamorgan County Record Office readily placed their knowledge and the resources of their repositories at my service. Dr. Frank Cumbers, former Book Steward of the Epworth Press, allowed me to make use of Curnock's edition of the Journal, and Dr. Bowmer was good enough to provide the copy for the photograph which appears as a frontispiece. Sir Hugo Boothby of Fonmon Castle, the owner of Wesley's letter to Mary Jones, and Miss Madeleine Elsas, the Glamorgan County Archivist, its present custodian, generously facilitated its reproduction as Plate 2, while I owe Plate 3—the portable pulpit which Wesley is said to have used at Bedwas, now at the Welsh Folk Museum, St. Fagans—to the kindness of the Curator, Dr. Iorwerth Peate. I hope to have another opportunity of thanking those individuals whose assistance related more to a forthcoming history of Wesley's Methodism in eighteenth-century Wales than to his Journal, but this is the place to express my gratitude to Mr. Colin Williams for making the maps, which are so essential to an understanding of the Journal, and to Mr. W. Kemmis Buckley, M.A., Llanelli, who cleared up the mystery of Wesley's 'Colonel St. Leger' and his home which had puzzled me for some time. Finally, I have to thank Dr. R. Brinley Jones, Director of the University of Wales Press, for the assiduous care he has devoted to the book all along.

A. H. WILLIAMS

Cardiff
January 1971

CONTENTS

MAPS

PLATES

ABBREVIATIONS

Arch. Camb. *Archaeologia Cambrensis.* The Journal of the Cambrian Archaeological Association.

Arm. Mag. *The Arminian Magazine.* vols. i–xx. London. 1778–97.

Bathafarn. The Journal of the Historical Society of the Methodist Church in Wales. vols. 1–25. 1946–70.

Brycheiniog. The Journal of the Brecknock Society. 1955 to date.

Cardiff MSS. 4.877. Extracts from the Diary of William Thomas, Michaelston-super-Ely, copied by David Jones, Wallington.

Christian History. *The Christian History,* or a General Account of the Progress of the Gospel in England, Wales, Scotland and America, as far as the Rev. Mr. Whitefield, his Fellow labourers and Assistants are concerned. London. ? 1742–47.

Corresp. and Minutes. *Correspondence and Minutes of the S.P.C.K. relating to Wales, 1699–1740.* Edited by Mary Clement. Cardiff. 1952.

Curnock. *The Journal of the Rev. John Wesley, A.M.* Edited by N. Curnock. Standard Edition. 8 vols. London. 1909–16.

D.N.B. *Dictionary of National Biography.*

D.W.B. *Dictionary of Welsh Biography down to 1940.*

E.M.P. *Early Methodist Preachers.* Edited by Thomas Jackson. 6 vols. London. 1871.

Er Clod. *Er Clod. Saith Bennod ar Hanes Methodistiaeth yng Nghymru.* Dan Olygiaeth Thomas Richards. Wrecsam. 1934.

Eurgrawn. *Yr Eurgrawn Wesleyaidd.* 1809 to date.

George Whitefield's Journals. *George Whitefield's Journals.* Published by The Banner of Truth Trust. 1960.

History of Brecknock. *A History of the County of Brecknock.* By Theophilus Jones. Enlarged by Sir Joseph Russell Bailey, Bart., First Baron Glanusk. Brecon. 1909–11.

Itinerary. *The Itinerary of Howell Harris, Trevecka.* Edited by M. H. Jones, and published as Supplements to *J.H.S.P.C.W.* below.

J.H.S.P.C.W. *The Journal of the Historical Society of the Presbyterian Church of Wales.* Caernarfon. 1916 to date.

Journal. *The Journal of the Rev. Charles Wesley, M.A.* Introduction and Occasional Notes by Thomas Jackson. 2 vols. London. n.d. (but Introduction is dated 7 March 1848).

Letters. *The Letters of the Rev. John Wesley, A.M.* Edited by John Telford. Standard Edition. 8 vols. London. 1931.

Life. The Life of the Rev. Charles Wesley, M.A. By Thomas Jackson. 2 vols. London. 1841.

Memorandum Book. The Memorandum Book of the Rev. Samuel Bradburn. 2 vols. in manuscript, now preserved at the Methodist Archives and Research Centre, London.

Meth. Mag. The Methodist Magazine. Vols. xxi–xliv. London. 1798–1821.

Min. of Conf. Minutes of the Methodist Conferences. Octavo edition. vols. 1 and 2. London. 1862.

N.L.W. Journal. The Journal of the National Library of Wales. Aberystwyth.

Origin. The Origin and History of Methodism in Wales and the Borders. By David Young. London. 1893.

Presenting Monmouthshire. The Journal of Monmouthshire Local History Council.

Rayer MSS. A list of Incumbents in the Diocese of Llandaff. Prepared by Mrs. Jenkins (later Mrs. Rayer), St. Athan's Rectory.

Sheriffs of Glamorgan. A List of the Names and Residences of the High Sheriffs of the County of Glamorgan from 1541 to 1966. Introduction by Richard John and Notes by George Williams. 1966.

S.T.L. (1742–1747). Selected Trevecka Letters (1742–1747). Transcribed and Annotated by Gomer M. Roberts. Caernarfon. 1956.

S.T.L. (1747–1794). Selected Trevecka Letters (1747–1794). Transcribed and Annotated by Gomer M. Roberts. Caernarfon. 1962.

Traf. Cym. Hanes Bed. Cymru. Trafodion Cymdeithas Hanes Bedyddwyr Cymru. 1901 to date.

Trans. Ang. Ant. Soc. Transactions of the Anglesey Antiquarian Society.

Trans. Carm. Ant. Soc. Transactions of the Carmarthenshire Antiquarian Society.

W. Wes. Meth. Welsh Wesleyan Methodism, 1800–1858. By A. H. Williams. Bangor. 1935.

Wesley. The Life and Times of the Rev. John Wesley, M.A. By L. Tyerman. 3 vols. 6th edition. London. 1890.

Whitefield. The Life of the Rev. George Whitefield, B.A. By L. Tyerman. 2 vols. 2nd edition. London. 1890.

W.H.S. Proc. The Proceedings of the Wesley Historical Society. 1897 to date.

Wesley Letters. Fonmon Collection. D/DF. Wesley Letters, at Glamorgan County Record Office.

Wes. Meth. Mag. The Wesleyan Methodist Magazine. London. 1822–78.

Y Pêr Ganiedydd. Y Per Ganiedydd (Pantycelyn). Gan Gomer Morgan Roberts. Cyf. 1. Llandysul. 1949; Cyf. 2. Aberystwyth. 1958.

INTRODUCTION

JOHN WESLEY (1703-91) made thirty-five specific visits to Wales between 1739 and 1790, and passed through the country on another eighteen occasions on his way to or from Ireland. Those visits and journeys had their origin, as did all his others throughout the British Isles, in an ordinary meeting of an ordinary Religious Society in Aldersgate Street, London, on 24 May 1738. On the evening of that day, this extraordinary man experienced the religious phenomenon known as conversion; he felt his heart 'strangely warmed', and received the assurance that his sins had been forgiven. The experience, at once so novel and so profound, transformed his life, so much so that he dedicated the remainder of his days to sharing it with others that they might acquire it themselves. The Methodist Awakening had been born, and it was only a matter of time before the Methodist Movement began to evolve, and, later still and after his death, the Methodist Church.

In the words of his brother Charles, who had passed through a similar experience a little earlier, what John Wesley had felt and seen on that May evening he told with confidence to others, and with astonishing results. He soon realized, however, that preaching of itself, or even when supported by fervent singing, was not enough. Something more was required if its results were not to be ephemeral: the opportunity, or rather regular opportunities, for those who had been converted—who 'felt the same way' as he and his brother now felt—to meet together to comfort and sustain each other in their newly acquired faith. The result was that small groups of converts began to meet together for this purpose, week by week, and the generic term applied to them all was 'society'. There were certain differences of nomenclature and of practice between the societies of England and those of Wales (for Howell Harris had also been converted as early as 1735), but they were in essence the same; the society-meeting was the natural response of like-minded men and women to a similar situation, the obvious answer to the common interests they now shared and the common problems they faced. It was as natural for such persons to join together for spiritual purposes in the eighteenth century as it is for like-minded people to unite for professional or social reasons today.

The society-meeting therefore followed the dramatic preaching as naturally as night follows day. But if any of the leaders in either country had any qualms about taking this step—about moving from converting to conserving, from winning to nurturing—and, in particular, if they were nervous of creating thereby a new 'movement' injurious to the Established Church, there was a valuable precedent to which they could have appealed, and to which indeed they did: the Religious Societies which had flourished within the Church since about 1678. These Societies consisted of small groups of godly people who 'lookt no further than the mutual Assistance and Consolation one of another in their Christian Welfare'. They laid great stress on strict attachment to the Church of England; on prayer, reading the Scriptures, singing psalms, partaking frequently of Holy Communion, and avoiding controversy; and on relieving the needs of the poor. As an organization they appear to have declined by 1738, but as isolated units or cells they were by no means extinct. It was to a meeting of such a society that John Wesley had gone on that 24th of May, and he doubtless knew of the similar society that had existed at Epworth before he was born. So with George Whitefield. 'I began to establish Religious Societies', he wrote; 'in the formation of these Associations I followed the Rules given by Dr. Woodward in a work written by him on the subject'. He formed such a society at Gloucester in 1735, before he was ordained; his first sermon after ordination was on 'The Necessity and Benefit of Religious Society'; on his voyage to Philadelphia in 1739 he wrote 'A Letter . . . to the Religious Societies lately set on foot in several parts of England and Wales' (which was soon translated into Welsh); and both he and the Wesleys were gladly received by the societies which already existed at Bristol and elsewhere.

The Religious Societies of Bristol illustrate what happened to many others in due course. There were at least five of them, and they were known by the name of the street in which they met: Nicholas Street, Baldwin Street, Gloucester Lane, Back Lane, and Castle Street. In parenthesis, as it were, it is interesting to recall that the Revd. Griffith Jones, Llanddowror, accompanied John Wesley to a meeting of the Castle Street society on 19 April 1739, and that the New Room in the Horsefair was originally built by Wesley, not to accommodate a *Methodist* society (for no such society existed then), but to provide better accommodation for the Religious Societies in Nicholas Street and Baldwin Street. In time, he introduced into these societies the love-feast and the watchnight services of the Fetter Lane Religious Society, and eventually, in February 1741, they became United Societies.

These and similar societies in other parts of England served Wesley's and Whitefield's purpose admirably at first. Here were groups of earnest men and women meeting regularly to supplement their worship in the local parish church, doing precisely what they were anxious that all their converts should do. It is not surprising, therefore, that both men visited them, encouraged others to join, and, where no such societies existed, established new ones themselves. They were opportunists in the best sense of the word, ready to use any and every appropriate means available to them, and easily the most appropriate were the Religious Societies first established in London and Westminster by a small group of young men who had listened to the sermons of Dr. Anthony Horneck and Mr. Smithies. They could hardly foresee that the consequences in the eighteenth century would differ so much from those in the seventeenth as to amount to a religious revolution.

John S. Simon, who devoted so much attention to this subject, traced the gradual evolution of the first Methodist society from the original societies of Dr. Horneck and Mr. Smithies. It is unnecessary to describe this development here, but it is relevant to note that whereas Horneck's societies were confined to members of the Church of England, the Orders drawn up, on 1 May and on later dates in 1738, for the society which first met at James Hutton's house in Little Wild Street, and later at Fetter Lane, contained no such restriction, though its Anglican members felt it their duty to attend the parish church, and to take Holy Communion there. In theory, therefore, this society was open to Anglicans and Dissenters alike. Nor was this something new (whether Simon realized it or not), for Dr. Woodward himself, a quarter of a century earlier, had stated that 'since the time that the Usefulness of these Societies has been visible to the World, their Zeal hath provoked some of their dissenting Brethren to join with them occasionally, and to set up the like among themselves'. Joseph Humphreys, for example, the son of a Dissenting minister at Burford in Oxfordshire, formed a Religious Society of 140 members at Deptford while a student barely 19 years of age at a Dissenting Academy. Nearer home, Henry Davies, Independent minister at Blaen-gwrach in Glamorgan, wrote to Howell Harris on 14 July 1739:

> I hear yt Esqr Jones of full moon is a man yt is truly inclin'd to piety, & very loving to assist those yt come together to keep Religious Societies thereabts.

'Esqr Jones of full moon'—Robert Jones, Fonmon Castle—was a good Anglican, despite his strong Puritan antecedents, but he and the evangelical Dissenter from Blaen-gwrach had a common interest in, and a warm sympathy with, the Religious Societies.

Howell Harris, like Whitefield, stated quite categorically that he began 'in imitation of the Societies which Dr. Woodward gave an account of in a little treatise he wrote on that head'. Whether that statement can be taken at its face value is open to question; the one which immediately followed it (to the effect that there were no other societies 'of the kind' in England and Wales at that time) was very wide of the mark. We know that Harris first began to establish societies as early as October 1736, and that he was given a copy of Woodward's *Short Account* in February 1739. It is much more likely that he 'began' at the suggestion of Griffith Jones, whom he had first met in May 1736 and who, as a member of the S.P.C.K. and the brother-in-law of Sir John Philipps, was well acquainted with the Religious Societies. But it is clear that he was at least aware of them, and that he deliberately set out to establish similar ones in Wales, though he preferred to call them 'Private Societies'. It is equally clear that the Revd. David Williams, the Dissenting minister in Cardiff, knew of them as well, for it was he who sent

Harris the copy of Woodward's 'little treatise'; indeed, he was very much involved in the Religious Society in Cardiff.

There were in Wales in 1738-9, as in England, a number of such societies. How many they were it is difficult to say, for the subject has not received the detailed study it deserves, but they were fairly numerous and there were several in south-east Wales—in precisely that part of the country nearest to Bristol. Some of them may have been formed by Anglicans, others by Dissenters, some were 'closed' while others were 'open' to Anglicans and Dissenters, but they all existed for a common purpose—in Sir John Philipps's phrase, 'to entertain one another in a Christian manner', or in Josiah Woodward's, 'that by their interchanged Counsels and Exhortations they might the better maintain their Integrity in the midst of a crooked and perverse Generation'. In time, doctrinal and other differences appeared, and members were obliged to make their choice—between the Calvinism of Whitefield and Harris and the Arminianism of the Wesleys, or between remaining within the Church and leaving it. Then, and only then, did Methodism become something rigid rather than fluid, a movement rather than an attitude to religion, and only then did the various labels begin to appear as some members and societies followed this leader and others that. Some became Arminian or Wesleyan, others Calvinist or Whitefieldian, while still others left Methodism and the Church and joined the ranks of Dissent.

At the same time, it is all too easy to ante-date this 'hardening' process. It occurred sooner in some places than in others, and it manifested itself earlier in certain individuals than in some societies. Some societies continued to invite preachers and exhorters from 'the other fold', while others refused to make a choice at all, preferring to adopt an attitude of benevolent neutrality towards all and sundry, provided they preached the Gospel of the Cross. The Cardiff society, for example, threw in its lot with John Wesley, and in this way an open Religious Society of Anglicans and Dissenters became the first Arminian or Wesleyan Methodist society in Wales. In November 1746 some of its members talked of breaking away from Wesley and sought Howell Harris's advice. Harris refused, and the refusal does him credit; 'as they had chosen Bro. Wesley', he wrote,

'I would advise them to go to him & be advis'd by him'. 'As they had chosen Bro. Wesley'; that is typical of what occurred in most of the Religious Societies of Wales—a deliberate act of choice. On the other hand, there were those who remained neutral. On his way through Glamorgan in December 1746 William Holland, the Moravian, called on his cousin John Holland at Aberthaw. Cousin John had been converted to Methodism by the Calvinist exhorter John Deer of St. Nicholas, and had then formed a Religious Society which met in his house. 'This Society', so William tells us, 'does not belong to either Mr. Wesley or Mr. Whitefield, tho' the latter and Mr. Howell Harris and the Rev'd Mr. Rowlands have leave to preach there whenever they come.' He adds: 'He [John] never could entirely agree in Opinion either with Mr. Wesley or Mr. Whitefield.' Nor could Thomas Prosser, who gave John Wesley and the Cardiff society so much trouble. No doubt he deserved Wesley's strictures; he had misled many members into quietism without possessing the necessary intellectual qualities of leadership—or so Wesley thought. Perhaps he was right. But the heart has its reasons no less than the head, a fact to which the logical Wesley was not always alive. On 28 September 1745 Prosser told Howell Harris that he could not 'but love them of both sides', for he was 'amongst them as one that is of none opinion'. Thomas Prosser's head may have been muddled, but his heart was sound. 'I am amongst them as one that is of none opinion'; not even Wesley could have cavilled at that, for in his classic definition, a Methodist was not 'a man of such or such an opinion', but 'one who has "the love of God shed abroad in his heart by the Holy Ghost given unto him"'. Someone, in fact, like Thomas Prosser, who evidently thought it of secondary importance that Paul had planted and Apollos had watered so long as God had given the increase. Or someone like John Holland, senior, an old man of 74 who welcomed all preachers 'who have the Glory of God & the Salvation of Souls at Heart'.

It is only against this background that John Wesley's early visits to Wales are intelligible. He came not to launch a new Movement, still less to establish a new denomination, but merely to give what help he could to Howell Harris in a common cause. It was as simple as that. This motive, moreover, not only brought him into the country; it determined his itinerary once he had come, for it was so planned (and planned *for* him not *by* him) as to embrace towns and villages where small groups of men and women had already adopted what Edmund Jones, the 'Old Prophet' and Dissenting minister of Pontypool, once (and so aptly) termed 'the Methodist way'. It is no longer necessary to infer this from the Journal, for we know that he and Harris often met at Newport for this specific purpose.

When Wesley first came, he came to what was probably, to him, a strange land. The suggestion that some of his ancestors had migrated to the Vale of Glamorgan from the ancestral home in Dorset is sufficiently plausible to merit investigation by the family genealogists, for there is more than one 'Westley' memorial in Llantwit Major church, and in 1740 George Westley, a yeoman from Llantwit, was admitted a freeman of Cardiff. But if Wesley was in fact related to any of these persons who shared with him the family name, and if, moreover, he had previously been in touch with them in person or by letter, he and they maintained a baffling silence. When he stepped into the boat at Aust at 10 o'clock on the morning of 15 October 1739, it is highly probable that he was crossing the Severn for the first time.

New and strange though the country itself may have been to him, however (and the surprise he expressed at its beauty tends to support this), he was by no means ignorant of its spiritual condition, or of the religious Awakening which was then under way, and which had preceded by some three years the similar Awakening in England for which he, with Whitefield, was so largely responsible. For the ties which linked South Wales to Bristol were closer then than they had ever been; the Old and the New Passages over the Severn were as popular in the eighteenth century as the railway through the Severn Tunnel became in the nineteenth, and as the Bridge over the river has become in our own day—and Bristol was the Mecca of Methodism in the west, as London was in the south-east and as Newcastle was soon to become in the north. There, centred on the harbour and the Hot Wells, as at Bath not so far away, a motley crowd of business men, men of fashion, and men of religion intermingled freely, and it was at one or other of the two places that Wesley had first met Griffith Jones and Howell Harris earlier in the year. Both men, it is safe to say, had opened their hearts to him about their work, and had thereby reinforced what George Whitefield had already told him about Wales. He was surprised by the natural beauty of the country between Chepstow and Abergavenny; he must surely have been well informed about the spiritual condition of its inhabitants.

He paid six visits between 1739 and 1742, and the places he visited reveal the influence of Howell Harris (at whose invitation he came) and the advice of his own brother Charles. For Charles Wesley had also been invited, and invited, rather oddly, by the Revd. Nathaniel Wells, rector of St. Andrew's, Dinas Powis, who, in March 1739, had had a sharp brush with George Whitefield while they were both awaiting the ferry at Aust. And yet it was he who, in November 1740, invited an equally zealous Methodist clergyman to Cardiff and to his own church. No satisfactory explanation of this *volte face* has yet been forthcoming, if there had been such a complete change of attitude at all; it may be that Wells disliked Whitefield more than his Calvinism, or his Calvinism more than his Methodism, and his fraternizing with Dissenters more than anything. Be that as it may, at this early stage in his rather chequered career, Nathaniel Wells (who disappeared from the Methodist stage as suddenly and as inexplicably as he had entered upon it) sympathized with the Wesleys, however much he disliked their friend and colleague, George Whitefield.

That first visit by Charles Wesley was followed by three others between July and September 1741, during which he visited the Calvinist societies at Llanishen, St. Nicholas, and Aberthaw, as well as the Arminian society in Cardiff. But their highlight was the friendship he struck with Robert Jones of Fonmon Castle who, in point of time, was the first of the gentry of Wales to come under the influence of Arminian Methodism and who, in the depth and sincerity of his religious convictions, was one of the most notable of them all. Already predisposed to religion (we recall his interest in the Religious Societies), he was converted in the Methodist sense of the word by Charles Wesley in July 1741. Thereafter he became a different person. He allowed a society to meet under his roof, transformed the dining room into a chapel, and ignored alike clerical gibes and peasant gossip about his new way of life. One can only surmise the difference it might have made to Methodism in Glamorgan, and even further afield, if the second Robert Jones had not been cut down in the flower of his manhood in 1742.

During the first three years, therefore, John Wesley, acting on the advice of Howell Harris and profiting from his brother's experience, visited a number of places in the counties of Monmouth and Glamorgan at each of which there were people who had adopted 'the Methodist way'. Some of them were clergymen: John Powell at Llanfaches, John Hodges and his curate Philip Thomas at Wenvoe, Nathaniel Wells at Dinas Powis, and John Richards at Porthkerry. Two of them, the squire of Fonmon and Thomas Price of Watford, were magistrates. And one was the rather formidable Elizabeth James, a widow who lived at Abergavenny, who is believed to have been related to Thomas Price, and who, in November 1741, became the wife of no less a Methodist than George Whitefield himself. With the exception of Robert Jones, and probably Hodges and Wells, all were Calvinists, but beneath the Calvinism of their heads lay the Methodism of their hearts, which enabled them to welcome anyone, irrespective of his doctrinal position, who shared with them a common faith and a common joy. John Wesley was as pleased to meet them as they were to hear him, for he came among them as the helpmeet of their leader and idol, Howell Harris.

In 1743 he broke new ground, this time in Breconshire, and as the result of another invitation, extended to him on this occasion by the Revd. Edward Phillips, rector of Maesmynys. A native of Llanfaredd near Builth Wells, and a graduate of Jesus College, Oxford, Phillips held the living of Maesmynys from 1740 until his death in 1777. How, where, and when he had met John Wesley, if indeed they had met at all (which is more than doubtful), we do not know, but once they had come face to face in May 1743 they took to each other immediately. That first visit to Builth was followed by three others during the next three years, during which he visited Maesmynys, Llansanffraid-yn-Elfael, Merthyr Cynog, Llan-ddew, and

Garth. Except possibly at Garth, there were Methodists gathered together in society at each of these places, and though no society met in Garth there was one at Bryn-ioau, the home-farm not far away. At Maesmynys there was Edward Phillips himself, at Llansanffraid the Revd. Rice Williams, at Llan-ddew the Revd. Thomas Lewis, and at Merthyr Cynog the exhorter John Price. Above all, there was Marmaduke Gwynne at Garth.

The wealthy heir to the patrimony of his grandfather, a judge on the North Wales Circuit, Marmaduke Gwynne set out one day to silence Howell Harris on what was probably his first visit to the Llangamarch district; instead, he was himself converted. That was in 1737. His conversion was no passing phase; on the contrary it went deep, so deep as to change his whole life. Thereafter he regularly heard Harris whenever he was within reach, and accompanied him on his way; he was ever ready to offer him a meal and, when necessary, a bed; he gave him advice, books, and ready cash from time to time, and expressed the hope that he would be ordained; he intervened decisively when Harris and some of his fellow Methodists were prosecuted for riotous assault at the Radnorshire Assizes in 1741, and again when Morgan Hughes, a Calvinist exhorter, was wrongfully imprisoned in Cardigan two years later; above all, it was he, more than anyone else, who helped Harris to overcome the parental objections to his marriage to Ann Williams of Skreen in 1744. Still more important for the Methodism of England (and ultimately for English church music), his own daughter Sarah (or Sally) married Charles Wesley in 1749. In later years, Sally claimed that the Methodists of Breconshire had escaped the bitter persecution endured by some of their fellows in England because of her father's active sympathy. That was too large a claim to make; they *were* persecuted from time to time, and Marmaduke Gwynne was not the only person of influence who took their part. But he undoubtedly exerted himself far more than anyone else on their behalf.

John Wesley, then, was first invited to Glamorgan and Monmouthshire by Howell Harris and to Breconshire by Edward Phillips, but it was the call of Ireland, conveyed to him by one of his own Preachers, Thomas Williams, which first took him as far as Anglesey. Information about Thomas Williams is not as plentiful as one would wish, but he was certainly a Welshman, and he may have been the son of that Thomas Williams of Llanishen Fach farm near Cardiff upon whom Wesley had called on 1 October 1741. By 1746 a Moravian society of some 500 members had been formed in Dublin, largely through the ministry of Benjamin La Trobe and John Cennick. During Cennick's absence in Germany, Williams arrived in Dublin and eventually persuaded many of the members to become Methodists. He then informed Wesley and urged him to pay them a visit. The journey which Wesley made in August 1747 was the first of sixteen on which he traversed Anglesey. Not one of them was a visit in the strict sense of the word; the island merely lay on his route to a more distant field. Moreover, he who lost no opportunity to preach wherever he might be, preached only on five of these journeys, and then merely because adverse winds had delayed his sailing from Holyhead.

He reached Anglesey for the first time at a most important juncture in its religious history. There were few counties in Wales so overwhelmingly Anglican, for the Puritan movement had passed it by, but in 1742 William Prichard, a member of the Independent congregation at Capel Helyg near Pwllheli, was evicted from his farm, Glasfryn Fawr, and moved to Anglesey. Towards the end of the year he was followed by Jenkin Morgan, another Dissenter, who formed a congregation of Independents at Caeau Môn in 1744, was ordained their minister in 1746, and had a chapel built at Rhos-meirch, near Llangefni, in 1748. Dissent had at last found a firm foothold in that corner of Wales. Meanwhile, Methodism had also made its appearance, though where and through whose influence it is difficult to say. But one of its earliest supporters was William Jones of Trefollwyn Blas, near Rhos-meirch, a man of some substance and education who, in later years, became a Moravian and finally an Antinomian. Methodist exhorters from other parts of Wales soon began to visit the island, as well as two Methodistical clergymen, Peter Williams and William Williams, Pantycelyn, and gradually the number of Methodists increased.

In short, the placid ecclesiastical waters of Anglesey were being stirred in the 'forties by Dissenters and Methodists, to the confusion of many and the alarm of not a few. Loyal Anglicans, who had hardly seen a Dissenter and had never set eyes on a Methodist, now saw too many of both—and too many at the same time, for Dissent and Methodism reached the island concurrently, and a Dissent, moreover, tinged with all the fire and enthusiasm of Methodism. Into this religious whirlpool came John Wesley in 1747—another Methodist, to be welcomed by all, by Jenkin Morgan the Dissenter as warmly as by William Jones the Methodist. On one occasion indeed, the Methodists and Dissenters of Anglesey had the rare privilege of hearing at one and the same meeting the founder of English Arminian Methodism and William Williams, Pantycelyn, the 'sweet singer' of the Calvinistic Methodism of Wales. As in south-east Wales and Breconshire, so in Anglesey; at Rhos-meirch, Bodlew, Rhyd-sbardun, Nantannog, Glan-y-gors, and similar places Wesley met small groups of 'hungry sheep' to whom he gladly preached, leaving it to others to gather them into their own doctrinal fold.

In the meantime, while he had thus been feeling his way tentatively into different parts of Wales over a period of some ten years or so, an event had occurred which had momentarily made him pause. In 1739, within a matter of weeks immediately prior or subsequent to his first visit, he had published his famous sermon on 'Free Grace', in which he had proclaimed the cardinal Arminian doctrine of universal salvation, the antithesis of the Calvinist doctrine of election. George Whitefield was on his way to Georgia at the time, where the nascent Calvinism to which he had already subscribed in England was reinforced by the writings of some Puritan divines and by Jonathan Edwards. But distant though he was from home, he was not unaware of the sermon and its publication; his friends saw to that, and in any case he had urged Wesley not to publish it before he set sail. Nor was he ignorant of other isolated events which exacerbated relations between Arminians and Calvinists, particularly the expulsion of one John Acourt from the Foundery, the Arminian citadel in London, and the displeasure caused to Arminians, and especially to Charles Wesley, by the publication of William Seward's Journal and its controversial Preface. In one letter after another from America, he implored

Wesley not to impair the harmony which had hitherto prevailed between them, but in vain, for however reluctant Wesley was to dispute publicly with him in person, he was almost constitutionally incapable of resisting the temptation to wage war against error—or what he regarded as error. And when, on 1 February 1741, he publicly tore up one of Whitefield's letters which had been published anonymously, and the next month expelled John Cennick from the Kingswood society, the die was cast. On 28 March 1741, a fortnight after Whitefield's return, the two friends separated, each to go his own way.

Howell Harris was no idle spectator of these developments; he regularly corresponded with Whitefield, and sympathized with John Acourt and John Cennick. He and his colleagues sided unequivocally with Whitefield in this doctrinal dispute, and Methodism in Wales as a result became Calvinistic rather than Arminian or Wesleyan. Relations between some of the leaders, and still more so between some of their followers, became very strained for a time, for one and all, great and small, were now obliged to make their choice. Thereafter, despite the efforts made to heal the breach by John Cennick, and particularly by Howell Harris (whose magnanimous spirit transcended his intellectual powers), orthodoxy assumed greater importance, and theological bickerings loomed large.

In the light of all this, John Wesley was obliged to reconsider his attitude to Wales. Hitherto he had been content and even happy to lend his Welsh friends a helping hand. Would they require such help henceforth, and if so, would it be welcome from him, tainted as he was with Arminianism? Howell Harris left him in no doubt; others might have their reservations, but to him, as to Wesley, Methodism was something far more important than Calvinism, Arminianism, or any other ism. He would continue to extend the right hand of fellowship, though he urged him to leave his sermon behind whenever he came to Wales. The result, as we have seen, was that although two distinct Methodist Movements now began to emerge, each with its societies, rules, officers, and official gatherings, Wesley continued to visit Wales. When he preached to the Methodists of Pontypool or Abergavenny, of Builth or Merthyr Cynog, he was preaching to Methodists of the other persuasion, and preaching by invitation. The invitations, and his response to them, do credit to one and all.

Nevertheless, given the zeal of some Methodists on both sides, a certain amount of misunderstanding, even friction, was perhaps inevitable. And such zealous persons were not wanting. There was Thomas Prosser who, if he proclaimed that he was 'of none opinion', held very decided views on some questions which bordered on the quietism (and possibly the Antinomianism) of the Moravians, and was by no means loath to propagate them among Arminians and Calvinists alike. Then there was the ubiquitous Henry Lloyd, known as Henry Lloyd of Rhydri though he was probably a native of Carmarthenshire. An admirable person again in many respects, and one who served the Arminian cause faithfully and well for half a century and more. But he, too, was of a restless spirit, and wandered in and out of Calvinist societies as he pleased. So, for that matter, did John Wesley. But Wesley *was* Wesley, and even so, he had done so only by invitation; it was one thing for the leader of English Methodism to visit Calvinist societies by request, it was quite another for one of his lay preachers to follow his example without so much as 'by-your-leave'. And finally, strange to say, there was Wesley himself, who had visited the Calvinists of Neath in 1746 and, wittingly or otherwise, had shaken some of them in their Calvinism. If that could happen at Neath, it could happen elsewhere—as in fact it had at far-off Plymouth. It was time to call a halt, so Harris thought, or at least to clear the air and come to some understanding. Had Wesley's lay preachers the right to preach to Calvinists as they pleased? And had the great man himself the right to propagate his Arminian views among them, and thereby sow the seeds of dissension and perhaps division?

These were some of the questions discussed at the Newcastle Emlyn Association of Welsh Calvinistic Methodism in January 1747, and again, a few days later, at a joint Association of the Calvinistic Methodism of England and Wales at Bristol, to which John Wesley and four of his Itinerant Preachers were invited. There the matter was amicably thrashed out. Thomas Prosser and Henry Lloyd were special cases, and were appropriately dealt with. More important was the general principle raised by Wesley's visit to

Neath. 'It was fear'd', so runs the report, 'that the consequences of Mr. Westley's preaching at Neath would be a separation in the Society.' Wesley made it clear that nothing had been further from his mind. He had had no intention of forming a society at Neath, nor would he do so wherever a Calvinist society already existed; on the contrary, he would exert all his influence to prevent dissension and secession. The Calvinists were reassured, and they in turn reassured him; he and his preachers would still be made welcome among them, provided their visits were made after prior consultation and in the spirit of the words he had just spoken. It was a sensible arrangement, a triumph of goodwill and common sense, a gentleman's agreement to live and let live.

How well it would have worked out, it is now impossible to say. John Wesley's Journal for the next three years, during which he preached in the main only in Anglesey, and then only by invitation, suggests that, as far as he was concerned, it might have worked well. On the other hand, there is some evidence to suggest that Howell Harris was still a little uneasy because of the misplaced zeal of some of Wesley's followers, and it is just possible that their unpredictable activities might, in time, have made it null and void. In the event, a domestic upheaval within Welsh Calvinistic Methodism made it superfluous.

Ever since 1746, the tension between Howell Harris and some of his colleagues in Wales (especially Daniel Rowland, William Williams, and Howell Davies) had been mounting. His heretical views on the Godhead of Christ (the doctrine of Patripassianism, the belief that God Himself had died on the Cross); his arrogance and, arising from it, his almost irrepressible itch to discipline and to rebuke; and his innocent but highly indiscreet consorting with Madam Sidney Griffith of Cefn Amwlch—all these factors eventually proved too much for some of his friends, who finally separated from him at the Llanidloes Association in May 1750, and met on their own at Llantrisant the following July. The Methodism of Wales was split from top to bottom.

John Wesley had neither the right nor the desire to intervene in this domestic dispute, but it was inevitably of some interest to him, for his relations with Welsh Methodists from the start had been based almost entirely on his personal relations with Howell Harris; it was he who had first invited him to Wales in 1739, and it was with him, as the acting Moderator of the Calvinistic Methodism of England and Wales, during Whitefield's absence in America, that he had made the Bristol Agreement in 1747. Now everything was changed; Harris, who was on the verge of a physical and nervous breakdown, had retired to Trefeca (where he was soon to establish his quasi-Moravian religious and industrial community or Family), and his place at the head of the Methodism of Wales had been taken by others. Wesley had once met Daniel Rowland in Monmouthshire and William Williams in Anglesey and had preached with both, but he had not met either since. He may have known that they had occasionally gently chided Harris about his close association with him, and about his long absences in England; they, for their part, must surely have known where his sympathies lay, however impossible he must have found it to endorse Harris's doctrinal deviations, or to condone his imperiousness. Whether they, and particularly Howell Davies, would have honoured, or felt themselves to be under an obligation to honour, a working agreement made by Harris on his own responsibility can only be surmised. More likely than not they decided to continue their remarkably successful work of converting sinners as before, indifferent to what was happening in England or to what John Wesley might do in Wales; they had their divine task to perform and he had his, and the less they had to do with each other the better. That is how they may have viewed the position; we simply do not know. If so, Wesley would not have dissented. He had had very little to do with Rowland or Williams, and nothing at all with Howell Davies; he lacked the necessary staff of Welsh-speaking Preachers through whom alone he could hope for success; and he had enough, and more than enough, to engage his attention and to consume his energies and resources in England, Scotland, and Ireland. Under the circumstances, he could happily leave Wales to the Welsh Methodists, Calvinists though they were, the more so as they were doing their work so well. That is how the situation may have appeared to him in the spring of 1750. What is certain, however, is this: though he kept in touch with the few societies he had in Wales through some of his Preachers, he himself paid only two specific visits to South Wales during the next twelve years, and one of those was made to resuscitate the society at Cardiff. But for two unforeseen developments, his visits thereafter might not have been any more frequent.

In the first place, in 1761 he sent one of his young Preachers, Thomas Taylor by name, to begin his ministry in Glamorgan. Taylor may not have been the first Preacher to be stationed there (the records for the previous years are very incomplete), but he was probably the first to introduce Arminianism into Gower and, later, into Pembrokeshire. The report which he gave Wesley at the Conference of 1763 so impressed him that he forthwith appointed an additional Preacher to Pembrokeshire, a decision which, in the fullness of time, led to the penetration of Wesleyan Methodism into the greater part of Wales.

Secondly, Howell Harris was reunited with his former colleagues and friends. During the long interval at Trefeca, and in the Breconshire Militia during the Seven Years War, he had never lost touch with the Wesleys, however isolated he may have been from his fellow Methodists in Wales. They had corresponded with each other; they had called on each other; and in 1760 (no doubt in his regimentals, for he travelled thither from Yarmouth), Harris attended Wesley's Conference in Bristol. The two brothers had always regretted his enforced retirement, and Charles had written a lengthy poem in which he had urged him to resume his evangelistic activities. That was in 1755. Now, in 1763, and again at Bristol, he and John were delighted to hear of his re-call and that he had already attended a Welsh Association the previous May. John Wesley can be excused if he now thought the *status quo* had been restored, and that he could therefore venture again into what, for some years, had appeared to be rather forbidding, if not actually forbidden, territory. Between them, the news of the promising pioneering work of Thomas Taylor (assisted, no doubt, by the revival of religion which broke out at Llangeitho in 1762 under the ministry of Daniel Rowland), and the equally cheering news that his old friend Howell Harris was back in the fray, may have convinced John Wesley that the time had come to pay more attention to Wales, and that he could do so without embarrassing himself or others.

From 1763 onwards, therefore, at least two Preachers were stationed in South Wales, and, in all, about 80 spent a year or more in the country between then and 1791, the year of Wesley's death. Very few of them make an appearance in the Journal, but it would be a travesty of history, as well as of justice, to forget that they were constantly in the background, accompanying Wesley whenever he visited their circuits, nurturing the societies and breaking new ground in the intervals in between. For the first few years they were officially stationed in Glamorgan and Pembrokeshire, but they took a generous, perhaps too generous, view of their responsibilities, and soon attempted to cover the country between Chepstow in the east and Dale in the west. Some of them also began to push northwards, and at one time the Breconshire Circuit embraced five counties and the whole, or the greater part, of three. Meanwhile, after 1763, when the Chester Circuit was first formed, the Methodism of Cheshire had overflowed into Wales, around Mold and Wrexham. The story of Methodism in north-east Wales, however, differs in some important respects from that elsewhere. It cannot be pieced together, even fragmentarily, from John Wesley's Journal or the *Minutes of Conference*; it was never a circuit within Wales but rather the extension of a circuit outside; except at Kinnerton and Bronnington, it was not the fruit of the labours of Methodist Preachers, but of a handful of exhorters or local preachers; and above all, it led, as it did nowhere else, to the creation of a Welsh-speaking section of the Methodist Church in 1800.

Success was limited for many years. When Wesley died, his Movement was represented by three circuits, seven Preachers, and about 600 members scattered between Roch in Pembrokeshire, Chepstow in Monmouthshire, and Mold in Flintshire; it was not until the last decade of the century that progress was at all rapid. Some of the Preachers who served Wesley were first-rate men. They included a few who later became eminent in Methodist history in Britain and overseas—men like Samuel Bradburn, Thomas Taylor, and Richard Whatcoat—and many more who, though they never achieved such eminence, laboured diligently and successfully according to their light. But there were others, raw and inexperienced young men whose achievements did not match their hopes, and whose zeal outshone their ability. Justice, however, compels one to add that the distances they were expected to cover were inordinately and unnecessarily long. Many parts of the country, especially anglicized south Pembrokeshire (where they might have expected more success) had been surfeited with preaching long before they came. They often lacked the vital assistance of a good staff of local preachers and class leaders, to supplement and consolidate their preaching and pastoral work during the intervals between their infrequent visits. They sometimes found it hard to enforce Methodist discipline, which was always strict and sometimes harsh. Above all, they found it increasingly difficult during the later years to combat the growing strength of Calvinism and the increasing menace of Antinomianism, because of their inability to preach in Welsh.

For Arminian Methodism, after all, was an English importation conducted predominantly in English among a population overwhelmingly Welsh. John Wesley once deplored 'the confusion of tongues', and his lack of Preachers who could speak and preach to the people in their native tongue, though it is doubtful whether he deployed the few who could to the best advantage. He himself may have hoped to add Welsh to the languages he had already mastered, for both he and his brother Charles subscribed to Thomas Richards's Welsh–English Dictionary. If so, and if he succeeded, he made no use of it, and it was left to one of his lieutenants, Dr. Thomas Coke, a native of Brecon, to suggest after his death that Welsh-speaking Preachers should be stationed in Wales, and in North Wales in particular. He carried the Conference of 1800 with him, with the result that, when the nineteenth century dawned, the Methodist Church in Wales (for it *was* a Church by then) was poised to take advantage, through the media of English and Welsh, of the rapid growth of population and all the other remarkable developments of the Victorian Age that was soon to dawn. That was something which Wesley in his wildest dreams could hardly have foreseen when he crossed the Severn on 15 October 1739 to get his first glimpse of Wales.

When John Wesley set out from Brecon to Carmarthen at 3 a.m. on Monday, 9 August 1790 on what proved to be his last visit to Wales, he had ample opportunity to reflect upon the changes he had seen since he had first visited the country half a century earlier—assuming, of course, that he could have spared the time for such mundane reflections from reading a book, writing letters, or preparing the next number of the *Arminian Magazine*. That he was travelling in a chaise and not on horseback would surely have been the first thing to strike him, and travelling along a road which had improved considerably in recent years. For many years he had traversed the greater part of the British Isles on horseback, and had had some unpleasant and even dangerous experiences. Those days were now over; since 1772, thanks to the generosity of some of his friends, he had had his own chaise, and even when he was unable to use it, there were the stage-coaches which, by now, were a common sight in the countryside.

To add to his comfort (or at least, to lessen his discomfort) new roads had been made and old ones improved. There were still far too many of the old and too few of the new, but the creation of Turnpike Trusts by private Acts of Parliament had wrought considerable improvement since the middle of the century. That road along which he was now travelling—the high road from Gloucester through Abergavenny and Brecon to Carmarthen—had already been improved, and so had others in different parts of Wales. True, such improvements had not been made without a considerable outlay of private money; a Turnpike Trust was a business concern, not a philanthropic institution, and the hard-headed men who sank their money in it expected a reasonable return. He and his Preachers were no more exempt from paying tolls than anyone else, though the local Methodist societies usually paid them on their behalf; in August 1784 John Church, the society-steward at Brecon, had paid 17*s*. 4*d*. to cover the tolls of the circuit Preachers to and from Beilïe, near Defynnog, during the previous two years, as well as 1*s*. 4*d*. for Wesley himself. But it was money well spent, and he could be sure the Methodists of Brecon did not begrudge it.

It would surely have occurred to him too that the country through which he was travelling was as beautiful as ever. When first he had seen it in 1763, he had remarked that no stretch of country in England was comparable to the fifty miles between Chepstow and Trecastle. It was still as beautiful, a pleasant change from the ugliness that was now sprawling over so many parts of industrial England. Such ugliness, he might have reflected, was remarkably rare in Wales; not merely the Towy valley through which he was then passing, but the greater part of Wales was still a sight to behold. There were, of course, ominous signs of change along the route he would be taking from Pembrokeshire, and indeed within that lovely county itself. But the collieries there were not to be compared with those in the north of England, either in size or number, and if more and more people were engaged in digging coals and smelting copper between Llanelli and Neath, they were not numerous as yet. Wales was still essentially rural. He may have heard something from Hugh Bold, the lawyer-Methodist at Brecon, about some iron furnaces in which he was interested on the other side of the mountain at a place called Merthyr Tydfil, but he had never been there himself.

Nor had the people changed perceptibly; they were as friendly as ever, and as Welsh, as so many of his Preachers had remarked from time to time. He had made good friends with many of them, even among the gentry, but by now many of them were no more. At quite an early date he had lost his good friend Robert Jones of Fonmon, but he had kept in touch with his widow Mary, and had seen her within a few weeks of her death some two years ago. Marmaduke Gwynne of Garth had also died; so had his wife, their eldest son Howell, and Howell's son Marmaduke. So, too, had Howell's brother-in-law, his own brother Charles. His widow was still alive, with the three children who had survived from their large family: Sarah, who had been given her mother's name, and of whom he was so fond, and her two musically gifted brothers, Samuel and Charles, though he was not at all happy about the public recitals they were giving to the élite of London. And there were the Vaughans of Trecwn and the Bowens of Llwyn-gwair, whom he would see within a few days, and by whom he would once more be made welcome.

The clergy had been no less friendly than the gentry. One or two had not shown that courage he would have admired by defying their ecclesiastical superiors and allowing him to preach in their churches. But that was a long time ago, and he had met with little or no outright opposition from any of them. Some of them, with the passing of time, had proved to be broken reeds—old John Hodges of Wenvoe, for instance, and the cryptical Nathaniel Wells. But in recent years, in Wales as in England, more clergymen had become more and more evangelical in their outlook and were always pleased to see him, especially David Pugh at Newport in Pembrokeshire, and Thomas and Edward Davies near Bridgend. True, nearly all of them were Calvinists, but evangelical Calvinists who must have reminded him of their predecessors, with whom he had found it so easy to co-operate in the early days: Edward Phillips, Rice Williams, Thomas Lewis, and John Powell. He had long since lost touch with them all—that Disruption within Welsh Methodism had a lot to answer for!—and most of them had probably gone to their reward; but it had been good to know them. As for the Calvinists of Wales in general, he had got on well with Daniel Rowland and William Williams on the one or two occasions on which they had met, and they might have found it possible to work more closely together if they had seen more of each other. But he had never been able to make much of Howell Davies; for some reason or other—perhaps it was his own Arminianism, or his trespassing on his preserve in Pembrokeshire—they had never been able to make good contact. With the layman Howell Harris, however, it had been a very different story. He had his weaknesses and limitations, to be sure, and some of his friends had complained about his autocratic nature, in much the same way as some of his own Preachers had complained about his. But he could not but admire and respect him, especially for the untiring efforts he had made over the years to reunite them all, Englishmen and Welshmen, Arminians, Calvinists, and Moravians; and though they had crossed verbal swords with each other time and again, they had remained firm friends to the end. Now he, too, was dead, but the community he had established at Trefeca lived on.

As for the people of Wales in general, most of those who had joined his societies belonged to the lower orders, but they were none the worse for that; so did some of his best Preachers. But there were others, endowed with more worldly goods, whom he had found most agreeable to meet and from whom he could always be assured of a warm welcome. The wheel of fortune had indeed turned! There was a time, he might have recalled, when he had been stoned and cursed, and when he could never be sure that he would escape with his life. All that was now past, and he was honoured and respected wherever he went. Whether he deserved such honour and respect, he may not have been so sure. Perhaps (he may have mused, as his chaise rumbled into the yard of the Red Lion in Carmarthen for tea) it was merely the honour and respect paid to old age. Or . . . was it?

But what of the Movement he had launched and guided for over fifty years? If the countryside was still pleasing, the people friendly, and he himself able to go his way in peace, what had he and his Preachers to show for their labours? Three extensive circuits and about 600 members. Nothing to be jubilant about, he must have thought, and certainly nothing to be complacent about. But then, there was another Methodist Movement in Wales, thoroughly Welsh-speaking (which his unfortunately was not) which, though as Calvinist as his old friend George Whitefield or that remarkable lady, the Countess of Huntingdon, could have wished, was far better organized than theirs, and accordingly far more successful. It was good to know that there were so many other Methodists in Wales, despite the doctrinal garb they wore, and the trouble which some of the more extreme among them had given his Preachers with their Antinomianism. For they had transformed the spiritual condition of the country. And that was really all that mattered.

Such are some of the reflections which might have passed through his mind on that August day as he travelled down the Towy valley. But if, before leaving Brecon, he could have spared a few hours to cross the mountains with Hugh Bold, or if, a few years earlier, he had spent a day or two around Wrexham, and had made a detour through Northop and Denbigh on his way back to Chester, he would have seen something which would have gladdened his heart. Merthyr Tydfil in South Wales, and Brymbo in the North, were symbolical of that industrial development which was soon to engulf large tracts of Wales, and present Wesleyan Methodism, in common with all the other religious organizations, with a great challenge and a glorious opportunity; Northop and Denbigh again were symbols of the medium through which the challenge could be met and the opportunity seized. Within a mere decade, the Movement which Wesley had striven for so long to keep within the confines of the Established Church had taken the fateful step of leaving it. But it had also taken the necessary measures to appeal to the people of Wales through their own language. He would have deplored the one; he would have been immensely cheered by the other. There would have been pleasure tinged with sadness if he could have foreseen the immediate future, no less than if he had taken a few minutes to recall the past.

JOHN WESLEY IN WALES

JOHN WESLEY IN WALES

I

15–20 OCTOBER 1739

Bristol · New Passage · Devauden · Abergavenny · Usk
Pontypool · Cardiff · Newport · Cardiff · Bristol

[Prior to this visit, John Wesley had doubtless been informed of the Religious Awakening in Wales by George Whitefield at Bristol on the previous 31 March; by Griffith Jones, Llanddowror, at Bath on 10 April, and at Bristol nine days later; and, above all, by Howell Harris at Bristol on 19 June. *vide Bathafarn*, xvi. 23–39.]

MONDAY, 15 OCTOBER 1739

4½, Writ to Fish, on business; 7, at Mr. Deschamps', tea, conversed, many tarried, singing, prayer; 8, set out with Deschamps, Williams;[1] *10, at the New Passage, wind high; 1, Chepstow; 2, set out, Devauden, Wr. Edwards's, singing, dinner, conversed; 3.45, upon the Green, 1 Cor. i, 30, 400;*[2] *5.30, at Mr. Nexey's; 5.45, Matt. v, 3, singing, etc; 7.45, conversed; 8.45, supper, conversed; 11.*

Upon a pressing invitation, some time since received,[3] I set out [from Bristol] for Wales. About four in the afternoon, I preached on a little green at the foot of Devauden (a high hill, two or three miles beyond Chepstow) to three or four hundred plain people on *Christ our wisdom, righteousness, sanctification and redemption.* After sermon, one who, I trust, is an old disciple of Christ, willingly received us into his house, whither many following, I showed them their need of a Saviour from those words, *Blessed are the poor in spirit.*

[1] John Deschamps and Anthony Williams were Bristol Methodists.
[2] Wesley's estimate of the number of his hearers.
[3] Doubtless from Howell Harris the previous June.

TUESDAY, 16

6½, Drest, prayer; 7.15, tea, conversed; 8, at the Green, Acts xvi, 30; 10, set out; 1.30, Abergavenny, within, dinner, Diary; 3, Col. iii, 22 etc; within, lots; 3.30, at Mr. Waters', within, Acts xxviii, 22, 1000; 5, at Mr. Waters', tea, conversed; 7, at Mrs. James', Acts v, 30 etc; 9, at Mr. Waters', supper, conversed, prayer; 10.30, Nanny, conversed, prayer; 11.

In the morning, I described more fully the way to salvation, *Believe in the Lord Jesus Christ and thou shalt be saved*. And then, taking leave of my friendly host, before two came to Abergavenny.

I felt in myself a strong aversion to preaching here. However, I went to Mr. W.[1] (the person in whose ground Mr. Whitefield preached) to desire the use of it. He said, 'With all his heart— if the minister[2] was not willing to let me have the use of the church'. After whose refusal (for I wrote a line to him immediately) he invited me to his house. About a thousand people stood patiently (though the frost was sharp, it being after sunset) while, from *Acts* xxviii, 22, I simply described the plain old religion of the Church of England which is now almost everywhere spoken against under the new name of Methodism. An hour after, I explained it a little more fully in a neighbouring house,[3] showing how *God hath exalted Jesus to be a Prince and a Saviour, to give repentance and remission of sins.*

WEDNESDAY, 17

6¼, Drest, prayer, read Life of Mr. Henry;[4] 7, at Mrs. James', conversed, tea; 8, Acts xvi, 30, 700; 9.30, at Mr. Waters', within; 10.30, set out; 12.30, Usk, at the Castle, dinner; 1, Matt. xviii,

[1] A Mr. Waters, a Presbyterian author of religious pamphlets who, on 5 Apr. 1739, had invited George Whitefield to Abergavenny and had erected a 'very commodious' stand at the back of his garden, from which Whitefield had preached. *George Whitefield's Journals*, 245. *N.L.W. Journal* x. 4.

[2] The Revd. Evan Eustance, vicar of Abergavenny 1719–76.

[3] The home of Mrs. Elizabeth James, a widow, in Cow Lane (now Nevill Street). On 14 Nov. 1741 Mrs. James married George Whitefield in St. Martin's church, Caerphilly.

[4] Matthew Henry (1662–1714), the eminent Nonconformist commentator and a native of Broad Oak near Worthenbury, Flintshire, not Philip Henry, his father, as in Curnock, ii. 294.

11; 2.15, set out; 3.30, Pontypool, Mr. Griffiths not [at home], at the Cock, tea; 4.15, at the School Steps, Acts xvi, 31, 600; 5.45, at Tho. Allgood's,¹ many tarried; 6.15, singing, etc; 8.30, supper, conversed; 10, prayer.

The frost was sharper than before. However, five or six hundred people stayed while I explained the nature of that salvation which is through faith, yea, faith alone; and the nature of that living faith through which cometh this salvation.² About noon I came to Usk, where I preached to a small company of poor people on those words, *The Son of Man is come to save that which is lost.* One grey-headed man wept and trembled exceedingly, and another who was there (I have since heard) as well as two or three who were at Devauden, *are gone quite distracted*; that is, they mourn and refuse to be comforted till they *have redemption through His blood.*

When I came to Pontypool in the afternoon, being unable to procure any more convenient place, I stood in the street and cried aloud to five or six hundred attentive hearers to *believe in the Lord Jesus* that they *might be saved.* In the evening I showed His willingness to save all who desire to come to God through Him. Many were melted into tears. It may be that some will *bring forth fruit with patience.*

THURSDAY, 18

6¼, Drest, prayer, Diary; 7.15, tea, conversed; 8.15, Rom. iv, 5, 400; 10, set out; 12, Newport, dinner, within;³ 1, set out, conversed; 3, Cardiff, at Mr. Tho. Glascott's,⁴ many tarried, conversed, tea; 5, at the Shire Hall, Acts xvi, 31; 6.30, at home, conversed; 7, at

¹ Probably the Thomas Allgood who developed the japanning industry at Pontypool and who, with his brother and son, established it at Usk in 1761. *D.W.B.*

² John Miles, a convert of Howell Harris, 'providentially' met Wesley at Abergavenny and accompanied him to Cardiff. He was very impressed, and found it difficult to believe that Wesley was an Arminian. *J.H.S.P.C.W.*, Supplement 10, 400–1 (where the letter is wrongly dated 24 Oct. 1740).

³ Possibly at the home of the parents of John Thomas, who was thrice mayor of Newport, for Wesley and Harris often met there 'to concert plans'. *Meth. Mag.*, 1813, 843–5.

⁴ Thomas Glascott, possibly a glazier by trade, an overseer of the poor, and a prominent member of the Cardiff society. J. H. Matthews, *Cardiff Records*, iii. 204, 444; *W.H.S. Proc.* iii. 176; *Bathafarn*, i. 28.

the Shire Hall, Matt. v, 3, 4; 8.45, at home, supper; 9.15, at society here,[1] conversed, prayer; 11.

I endeavoured to cut them off from all false supports and vain dependencies by explaining and applying that fundamental truth *To him that worketh not, but believeth on Him that justifieth the ungodly, his faith is counted to him for righteousness.*

When we were at Devauden on Monday, a poor woman who lived six miles off came thither in great heaviness. She was deeply convinced of sin and weary of it, but found no way to escape from it. She walked from thence to Abergavenny on Tuesday, and on Wednesday from Abergavenny to Usk. Thence, in the afternoon, she came to Pontypool where, between twelve and one in the morning, after a sharp contest in her soul, our Lord got unto Himself the victory; and the love of God was shed abroad in her heart, testifying that her sins were forgiven her. She went on her way rejoicing to Cardiff, whither I came in the afternoon. And about five (the minister not being willing I should preach in the church on a week-day),[2] I preached in the Shire Hall (a large convenient place)[3] on *Believe and thou shalt be saved.* Several were there who laboured much to make a disturbance, but our Lord suffered them not. At seven I explained to a much more numerous audience the blessedness of mourning and poverty of spirit. Deep attention sat on the faces of the hearers, many of whom, I trust, *have believed our report.*

FRIDAY, 19

6½, Drest, prayer; 7, tea, conversed; 8.15, set out with Glascot, etc; 10.15, Newport, Acts xvi, 30; 12.30, set out; 2.45, Cardiff; 3, within, ate; 3.45, Shire Hall, Rom. xiv, 17!; 5.15, at home, dinner; 6, at the Shire Hall, Matt. v, 5 etc; 9, at Mr. Philips's,[4] supper, conversed, prayer; 11.15.

[1] For the origins of the Cardiff Religious Society, which developed into the first Arminian Methodist society in Wales, *vide Bathafarn*, xv. 25-44; xvii. 34-8; xviii. 42-51.

[2] The Revd. Thomas Colerick, vicar of St. John's church 1718-61.

[3] The Shire Hall stood in the grounds of Cardiff castle, the Town Hall in the High Street; both have now been demolished. Wesley often preached from the steps of the stone keep of the motte-and-bailey-castle.

[4] Probably Captain Phillips, who brought Charles Wesley over from Bristol on his first visit to Cardiff in Nov. 1740.

I preached in the morning at Newport on *What must I do to be saved?* to the most insensible, ill-behaved people I have ever seen in Wales. One ancient man, during a great part of the sermon, cursed and swore almost incessantly and towards the conclusion took up a great stone, which he many times attempted to throw. But that he could not do. Such the champions! such the arms against field-preaching!

At four I preached at the Shire Hall of Cardiff again, where many gentry, I found, were present. Such freedom of speech I have seldom had as was given me in explaining those words, *The kingdom of God is not meat and drink, but righteousness and peace and joy in the Holy Ghost.* At six, almost the whole town (I was informed) came together, to whom I explained the six last Beatitudes, but my heart was so enlarged I knew not how to give over, so that we continued there three hours. O! may the seed they have received have its fruit unto holiness and, in the end, everlasting life!

SATURDAY, 20

6½, Prayer, drest; 7, at Mr. Howel's,[1] many tarried, tea, conversed, prayer; 8, set out with Williams and Deschamps; 11.30, at the Rock,[2] dinner; 12.45, set out; 1.45, at the New Passage, Diary; 4, set out, conversed; 5.30. . . .

I returned to Bristol. I have seen no part of England so pleasant for sixty or seventy miles together as those parts of Wales I have been in. And most of the inhabitants are indeed *ripe for the gospel.* I mean (if the expression appear strange) they are earnestly desirous of being instructed in it, and as utterly ignorant of it they are as any Creek or Cherokee Indians. I do not mean they are ignorant of the name of Christ. Many of them can say both the Lord's Prayer and the Belief. Nay, and some all the Catechism. But take them out of the road of what they have learned by rote, and they know no more (nine in ten of those with whom I conversed) either of gospel salvation or of that faith whereby alone we can be saved than

[1] Earlier in the year a Mrs. Howells of Cardiff had urged the Revd. David Williams, minister of Womanby Street Independent church, to invite Howell Harris to meet the members of the Cardiff Religious Society at her house. *J.H.S.P.C.W.*, Supplement 5, 159.　　　　　　　　　　　　　　　　　　　　　[2] In Chepstow.

Chicali or Tomo-chachi.[1] Now what spirit is he of, who would rather these poor creatures should perish for lack of knowledge than that they should be saved, even by the exhortations of Howell Harris or an itinerant preacher?[2]

II

7–12 APRIL 1740

Bristol · New Passage · Llanfaches · Pontypool · Llanhilleth
Cardiff · Watford · Llantarnam · Penrheol · Llanfaches
Bristol

MONDAY, 7 APRIL 1740. At the pressing instance of Howell Harris,[3] I again set out for Wales. In the evening I preached repentance and remission of sins at Llanfaches,[4] three miles from the New Passage.[5]

TUESDAY, 8. I preached at Pontypool on *By grace ye are saved through faith*, and in the evening at Llanhilleth, three miles from thence, on *I know that in me dwelleth no good thing*.

[1] Tomo-chachi, chief of the Indians of the Lower Creek, Georgia, whom Wesley had met in Georgia and whom J. E. Oglethorpe, founder of the colony, had brought back to England in 1734 and had presented to George II.

[2] Itinerant preaching by laymen and by clergymen outside their own parishes were, of course, two of the main charges levelled against the Methodists.

[3] Howell Harris had invited him by letter on 1 Feb. 1740. The doctrinal rift had not yet occurred, but Wesley's sermon on 'Free Grace' had already appeared, and feeling between Arminians and Calvinists was beginning to run high, especially at Bristol.

[4] If John Powell, the Methodistical rector of Llanmartin and Wilcrick, was curate of Llanfaches in 1740 (as he undoubtedly was in 1771) this probably explains Wesley's visits to the village, *post*, p. 10 n. 3 and *J.H.S.P.C.W.* xli. 71.

[5] There were two Passages over the Severn in the eighteenth century, which effectively linked Bristol and South Wales: the Old Passage (from Beachley to Aust) and the New (from Black Rock, Sudbrook, to Chiswell Pill). The New Passage belonged to the Lewis family of St. Pierre near Chepstow, and for the greater part of the century the tenant (who rented the ferry, the inn, and the fishery) was John Hoggard. The inn at Beachley was known as 'The Ostrich', that at Sudbrook at different times as 'New Passage House' and 'Black Rock'. The New Passage ferry ceased to operate in 1887, the Old in 1966 with the opening of the Severn Bridge. J. Bradney, *A History of Monmouthshire*, iv. Part 1, 32–3, 106–8; Ivor Waters, *Inns and Taverns of the Chepstow District*, 72.

WEDNESDAY, 9. After reading prayers in Llanhilleth church,[1] I preached on those words, *I will heal their backsliding, I will love them freely*. In the afternoon Howell Harris told me how earnestly many had laboured to prejudice him against me, especially those who had gleaned up all the idle stories at Bristol and retailed them in their own country. And yet these are good Christians! These whisperers, tale-bearers, backbiters, evil-speakers! Just such Christians as murderers or adulterers. *Except ye repent, ye shall all likewise perish*. In the evening I expounded at Cardiff the story of the Pharisee and the publican.

The next day, THURSDAY the 10th, after preaching thrice, I rode to Watford,[2] five miles from Cardiff, where a few of us joined together in prayer and in provoking one another to love and good works.

FRIDAY, 11. I preached in Llantarnam church on *By grace ye are saved through faith*. In the afternoon I preached at Penyrheol near Pontypool. A few were cut to the heart, particularly Mrs. A . . . d,[3] who had some time before given me up for a Papist, Mr. E . . . s[4] the curate having averred me to be such upon his personal knowledge at her house in Pontypool. I afterwards called *O ye dry bones, hear the word of the Lord*. And there was a shaking indeed. Three or four came to me in such mourning as I had hardly seen, as did a poor drunkard between eleven and twelve who was convinced by the word spoken on Tuesday.

[1] The living of Llanhilleth was apparently vacant from 1661 to 1741, but John Powell may have served as curate there as well as at Aberystruth until Oct. 1742, when, according to Howell Harris, he was 'cast out'; meanwhile, he had received the living of Llanmartin. Rayer MSS.; *D.W.B.*, s.n.; T. Beynon, *Howell Harris, Reformer and Soldier*, 44.

[2] Plas Watford, above Caerphilly, the home of Thomas Price, a Justice of the Peace, one of the original nine partners who founded the Dowlais Iron Company on 19 Sept. 1759, and a Calvinistic Methodist exhorter. Here some of the leaders of Calvinistic Methodism stayed in Jan. 1743 during the first joint Association of English and Welsh Calvinistic Methodism, held partly in the 'New Room' at Groeswen and partly here, when George Whitefield was appointed Moderator.

[3] Probably the wife of Thomas Allgood, at whose house Wesley called on 17 Oct. 1739.

[4] On 13 July 1739 the Revd. Edmund Jones, Independent minister at Pontypool, had informed Howell Harris that 'Evans of Pont y Poole still continues to persecute and I am afraid will blast the hopeful beginnings there'. *J.H.S.P.C.W.*, Supplement 6, 193.

SATURDAY, 12. After preaching at Llanfaches in the way, in the afternoon I came to Bristol.

III

I–7 OCTOBER I74I

Bristol · Newport · Llanishen · Fonmon · Cardiff · Pontypool
Abergavenny · Pontypool · Watford · Fonmon · Porthkerry
Bristol

[This was Wesley's first visit to Wales after the doctrinal break with Whitefield the previous March. He was accompanied on the first part of the journey by Robert Jones, Fonmon, who had returned to Bristol with Charles Wesley on 19 September.]

THURSDAY, 1 OCTOBER 1741. We set out for Wales, but missing our passage over the Severn in the morning, it was sunset before we could get to Newport. We enquired there if we could hire a guide to Cardiff, but there was none to be had. A lad coming in quickly after, who was going (he said) to Llanishen, a little village two miles to the right of Cardiff, we resolved to go thither.[1] At seven we set out. It rained pretty fast and, there being neither moon nor stars, we could neither see any road nor one another, nor our own horses' heads. But the promise of God did not fail. He gave his angels charge over us, and soon after ten we came safe to Mr. Williams' house at Llanishen.[2]

FRIDAY, 2. We rode to Fonmon Castle. We found Mr. Jones' daughter[3] ill of the small-pox, but he could cheerfully leave her and all the rest in the hands of Him in whom he now believed. In

[1] Now a suburb of Cardiff.

[2] Thomas Williams of Llanishen Fach farm (not of Blew House, as in Curnock, ii. 505 n. 3) was a member of a very prominent family in the Vale of Glamorgan, and was for some years one of Wesley's exhorters. He died 19 Apr. 1783, aged 86. T. J. Hopkins in *Vale of History* (ed. Stewart Williams), 110–12; *Bathafarn*, ix. 44.

[3] Robert Jones (1706–42) had two sons (one of whom, Samuel, was born posthumously and died within a year) and four daughters. This daughter was Catherine, then aged five; she survived to marry John Coghlan of Bristol. *Bathafarn*, xxv. 46.

the evening I preached at Cardiff in the Shire Hall, a large and convenient place, on *God hath given unto us eternal life and this life is in His Son*. There having been a feast in the town that day, I believed it useful to add a few words upon intemperance. And while I was saying, 'As for you, drunkards, you have no part in *this* life, you abide in death, you choose death and hell', a man cried out vehemently, 'I am one, and thither I am going'. But I trust God at that hour began to show him and others *a more excellent way*.

SATURDAY, 3. About noon we came to Pontypool. A clergyman stopped me in the first street; a few more found me out soon after, whose love I did not find to be cooled at all by the bitter adversaries who had been among them. True pains had been taken to set them against my brother and me by men who *know not what manner of spirit they are of*.[1] But instead of disputing we betook ourselves to prayer, and all our hearts were knit together as at the first.

In the afternoon we came to Abergavenny. Those who are bitter of spirit had been here also, yet Mrs. James (now Mrs. Whitefield)[2] received us gladly, as she had done aforetime. But we could not procure even two or three to join with us in the evening beside those of her own household.

SUNDAY, 4. I had an unexpected opportunity of receiving the Holy Communion.[3] In the afternoon we had a plain, useful sermon on the Pharisee and the Publican praying in the temple, which I explained at large in the evening to the best-dressed congregation I have ever yet seen in Wales. Two persons came to me afterwards who were, it seemed, convinced of sin and groaning for deliverance.

MONDAY, 5. I preached in the morning at Pontypool to a small but deeply attentive congregation. Mr. Price[4] conducted us from

---

[1] One of the Wesleys' critics was probably Edmund Jones, Pontypool. But time may have mellowed his attitude, for the Revd. J. Wilstead, Porthcawl, informs me that he has a book sent by John Wesley to Edmund Jones in 1764.

[2] This portion of Wesley's Journal was not published until 1749; hence the phrase in parenthesis.

[3] In St. Mary's Priory Church.

[4] Thomas Price, Watford was less contentious than many; on 8 Aug. he had advised Harris to beware of 'endless & drie disputings'.

thence to his house at Watford. After resting here an hour, we hastened on and came to Fonmon, where I explained and enforced those words, *What must I do to be saved?* Many seemed quite amazed while I showed them the nature of salvation and the gospel way of attaining it.

TUESDAY, 6. I read prayers and preached in Porthkerry church.[1] My text was *By grace are ye saved through faith.* In the evening, at Cardiff, I expounded *Zechariah*, iv, 7: *Who art thou, O great mountain? Before Zerubbabel thou shalt become a plain. And he shall bring forth the headstone thereof with shoutings, crying Grace, grace unto it.* The next morning we set out, and in the evening praised God with our brethren in Bristol.

IV

15–21 OCTOBER 1741

Bristol · New Passage · Wilcrick · Magor · Llanmartin
Machen · St. Bride's · Cardiff · Fonmon · Wenvoe · Porthkerry
Cardiff · Newport · Caldicot · Bristol

THURSDAY, 15 OCTOBER 1741. I was preparing for another journey to Wales, which I had designed to begin on Friday, when I received a message from H. Harris,[2] desiring me to set out immediately and meet him near the New Passage. I accordingly set out at noon, but, being obliged to wait at the water-side, did not reach Wilcrick[3] (the place he had appointed for our meeting) till an hour

---

[1] The living of Porthkerry was in the gift of Robert Jones, Fonmon. The incumbent from 1728 to 1757 was the Revd. John Richards, whose suspicions of Methodism were dispelled after he had heard Charles Wesley preaching there on 15 July 1741. Jackson, *Journal*, i. 287; Rayer MSS.

[2] The purpose of this visit was to attempt to reunite Arminian and Calvinistic Methodism.

[3] The rector of Llanmartin and Wilcrick (the two livings generally went together) from Feb. 1740 until his death in 1795 (in 1799 according to the Rayer MSS.) was the Revd. John Powell, who was in full sympathy with Methodism and who attended the joint English and Welsh Association at Watford in Jan. 1743. *D.W.B.*, s.n.; Rayer MSS.; *J.H.S.P.C.W.*, Supplement 7, 228–9, 240–1; Supplement 8, 273.

or two after night. But this was soon enough, for he had not been there nor could we hear anything of him. So we went back to Magor[1] and thence, in the morning, to Llanmartin, a village two miles off, where we heard Mr. Daniel Rowland was to be, and whom we accordingly found there. Evil surmisings presently vanished away and our hearts were knit together in love.[2] We rode together to Machen (five miles beyond Newport) which we reached about twelve o'clock. In an hour after, H. Harris came and many of his friends from distant parts.[3] We had no dispute of any kind, but the spirit of peace and love was in the midst of us. At three we went to church.[4] There was a vast congregation, though at only a few hours' warning. After prayers I preached on those words in the Second Lesson, *The Life which I now live, I live by faith of the Son of God, who loved me, and gave Himself for me.* Mr. Rowland then preached in Welsh on Matt. xxviii, 8, *Fear ye not, for ye seek Him that was crucified.*

We rode afterwards to St. Bride's-in-the moors,[5] where Mr. Rowland preached again. Here we were met by Mr. Humphreys and Thomas Bissicks of Kingswood.[6] About eleven, a few of us retired in order to provoke one another to love and to good works. But T. Bissicks immediately introduced the dispute and others seconded him. This H. Harris and Mr. Rowland strongly withstood but, finding it profited nothing, Mr. Rowland soon withdrew. H. Harris kept them at bay till about one o'clock in the morning.

[1] The first edition of the Journal has 'Mather', which suggests Mathern. But Curnock substituted Magor, and probably rightly so, for whereas Llanmartin is about two miles from Magor it is about nine from Mathern. Here perhaps it may be noted that Wesley's estimates of the distance between two places or of the mileage he covered are not always very accurate—even in terms of the so-called 'Welsh mile', which was longer than the British statute mile. Llanfaches, for example, which he visited on his second journey, is nearer 6 miles from the New Passage than 3.

[2] This is the only reference in the Journal to Wesley's meeting Daniel Rowland, Llangeitho, and it is difficult to understand Curnock's comment that it marked 'the beginning of a warm friendship'. Op. cit. ii. 508 n. 2.

[3] Including Herbert Jenkins, Thomas Price, and Mrs. Elizabeth James. *Bathafarn,* x. 43.

[4] St. Michael's church, Lower Machen.

[5] The village is St. Bride's Wentloog, the church (if indeed the service was held in it) St. Bridget's.

[6] Joseph Humphreys, an erstwhile Arminian, had broken with John Wesley in Apr. 1741; Thomas Bissicks had sided with John Cennick when Cennick parted with Wesley at Kingswood on 7 Mar.

I then left them and Capt. T. together.[1] About three they left off just where they began.

SATURDAY, 17. Going to a neighbouring house, I found Mr. H. and T. Bissicks tearing open the sore with all their might. On my coming in all was hushed, but Mrs. James of Abergavenny (a woman of candour and humanity) insisted that 'those things should be said to my face'. There followed a lame piece of work, but although the accusations brought were easily answered, yet I found they left a soreness on many spirits. When H. Harris heard of what had passed he hasted to stand in the gap once more, and with tears besought them all 'to follow after the things that make for peace'. And God blessed the healing words which he spoke, so that we parted in much love, being all determined to let controversy alone and to preach Jesus Christ and Him crucified.

I preached at Cardiff at three, and about five set out thence for Fonmon Castle. Notwithstanding the great darkness of the night, and our being unacquainted with the road, before eight we came safe to the congregation, which had been some time waiting for us.

SUNDAY, 18. I rode to Wenvoe.[2] The church was thoroughly filled with attentive hearers while I preached on those words, *Whom ye ignorantly worship, Him declare I unto you*. In the afternoon, I read prayers and preached at Porthkerry. In the evening there was a great concourse of people at the Castle,[3] to whom I strongly declared *the hope of righteousness which is through faith*.

---

[1] Captain Joseph Turner of Bristol, who sometimes accompanied Wesley on his travels.

[2] The rector of Wenvoe was the Revd. John Hodges (1700?–1777). He had first come into contact with English Methodism through Charles Wesley, whom he met on 7 Nov. 1740. He may have been the means of bringing the Wesleys into touch with Robert Jones, and John Wesley thought sufficiently highly of him to invite him to his first three Conferences, though he did so on the first occasion at Howell Harris's suggestion. Howell Harris stated (not later than 1743, and probably in May 1742) that Hodges administered Holy Communion every Sunday, catechized every Sunday afternoon, and kept a society in his church every Sunday evening. He seems to have come under the influence of mysticism in his later years and to have lost his early interest in Methodism, though Howell Harris dined with him and Mrs. Mary Jones at Fonmon as late as 14 July 1769. William Thomas the diarist, recording his burial on 5 Apr. 1777, added: 'Troubled with gout . . . a charitable man'. *D.W.B.*, s.n.; *J.H.S.P.C.W.* xxxiv. 47; Roberts, *S.T.L.* (*1742–47*) 54, 56; Beynon, *Howell Harris, Reformer and Soldier*, 25; *Cardiff MSS.* 4. 877; *The Christian History*, ii. 26–30.

[3] i.e. Fonmon Castle, not Cardiff Castle (as in Curnock, ii. 510 n. 4).

MONDAY, 19. I preached once more at Porthkerry and in the afternoon returned to Cardiff and explained to a large congregation *When they had nothing to pay, he frankly forgave them both.*

TUESDAY, 20. At eleven, I preached at the prison on *I came not to call the righteous but sinners to repentance.* In the afternoon I was desired to meet one of the honourable women, whom I found a mere sinner, groaning under the mighty hand of God. About six, at Mr. W's[1] desire, I preached once more on those words, *Whom ye ignorantly worship, Him declare I unto you.*

WEDNESDAY, 21. I set out after preaching, and about nine came to Newport. A clergyman, soon after I was set down, came into the next room and asked aloud, with a tone unusually sharp, 'Where those vagabond fellows were?'. Captain T. without any ceremony took him in hand, but he soon quitted the field and walked out of the house. Just as I was taking horse, he returned and said, 'Sir, I am afraid you are in a wrong way. But if you are right, I pray God to be with you and prosper your undertakings.'[2]

About one I came to Caldicot and preached to a small attentive company of people on *Blessed are they which do hunger and thirst after righteousness for they shall be filled.* Between seven and eight we reached Bristol.[3]

V

1–6 MARCH 1742

Bristol · Cardiff · Wenvoe · Fonmon · Bonvilston
Llantrisant · Cardiff · Llanishen · Cardiff · Bristol

SUNDAY, 28 FEBRUARY, 1742. In the evening I set out [from Bristol] for Wales. I lay that night about six miles from

---

[1] Probably the Revd. Nathaniel Wells, rector of St. Andrew's, Dinas Powis, who first invited Charles Wesley to Cardiff in Nov. 1740. *Bathafarn*, xv. 39–42; xvii. 27–33.

[2] Possibly the incumbent of St. Woollo's; if so, the Revd. Thomas Mills Hoare, M.A., who held the living from 1726 to 1759. Rayer MSS.

[3] Wesley was seriously ill immediately after returning to Bristol—not, as Captain Turner thought, because of a damp bed at St. Bride's Wentloog but as a result of 'riding continually in the cold and wet nights and preaching immediately after'. Telford, *Letters*, i. 358.

Bristol and preached in the morning, MARCH 1, to a few of the neighbours. We then hastened to the Passage but the boat was gone half an hour before the usual time so I was obliged to wait till five in the afternoon. We then set out with a fair breeze, but when we were nearly half over the river the wind entirely failed. The boat could not bear up against the ebbing tide but was driven down among the rocks, on one of which we made shift to scrabble up; whence, about seven, we got to land.

That night I went forward about five miles and the next morning to Cardiff. There I had the pleasure of meeting Mr. Jones of Fonmon, still pressing on into all the fullness of God. I rode with him to Wenvoe. The church was thoroughly filled while I explained the former part of the Second Lesson concerning the barren fig-tree, and the power of the Lord was present both to wound and to heal.

I explained in the evening at Fonmon, though in weariness and pain, how Jesus saveth us from our sins. The next morning at eight I preached at Bonvilston, a little town four miles from Fonmon.[1] Thence I rode to Llantrisant and sent to the minister[2] to desire the use of his church. His answer was, 'He should have been very willing but the bishop had forbidden him'.[3] By what law? I am not legally convicted either of heresy or any other crime. By what authority then am I suspended from preaching? By bare-faced arbitrary power. Another clergyman immediately offered me his church, but it being too far off I preached in a large room, spent a little time with the society[4] in prayer and exhortation, and then took horse for Cardiff.

[1] Hardly a 'town'! The village of Bonvilston stands on the A. 48, some seven miles west of Cardiff.

[2] Revd. Richard Harris, vicar of Llantrisant from 1728 to 1766; he succeeded James Harris, the main supporter of the S.P.C.K. in Glamorgan. (M. Clement, *Corresp. and Minutes*, 3 n. 16). Charles Wesley had found Richard Harris 'exceeding civil' on 17 Nov. 1740; though efforts had been made to persuade him to refuse him his pulpit, he refused to break his word. Jackson, *Journal*, i. 258.

[3] John Gilbert, bishop of Llandaff 1740–8.

[4] Probably a Welsh Calvinistic Methodist society, though an Arminian society was formed some time before Apr. 1749. Llantrisant was an important centre for the Calvinist societies of the district and one of the most prominent local exhorters was Howell Griffith of Trefeurig Uchaf, Llantrisant. The society met at his house and at Rhagat, the home of his tenant. *J.H.S.P.C.W.* xxxvii. 54–7.

THURSDAY, 4. About noon I preached at Llanishen and was afterward much refreshed in meeting the little earnest society.[1] I preached at Cardiff at seven on *Be not righteous overmuch* to a larger congregation than before, and then exhorted the society to fear only the being overwicked or the falling short of the full image of God.

FRIDAY, 5. I talked with one who used frequently to say, 'I pray God I may never have this new faith. I desire that I may not know my sins forgiven till I come to die'. But as she was some weeks since reading the Bible at home, the clear light broke in upon her soul. She knew all her sins were blotted out and cried aloud, 'My Lord and my God'. In the evening I expounded *This is the victory that overcometh the world, even our faith.* We afterwards admitted several new members into the society and were greatly comforted together.[2]

SATURDAY, 6. I left Cardiff and about eight in the evening came to Bristol.

VI

5–7 JULY 1742

Bristol · Cardiff · Fonmon · Henbury · Bristol

MONDAY, 5 JULY 1742. I rode to Cardiff [from Bristol] and found much peace and love in the little society there.

[1] This, too, may have been a Calvinistic Methodist society; the majority of its members were certainly predestinarians when Charles Wesley preached to them on 16 July 1741 (Jackson, *Journal*, i. 287). Whether it developed into an Arminian society later, or whether there were two societies in Llanishen, the one Calvinist and the other Arminian, it is impossible to say. For early Arminian Methodist societies in and around Cardiff, *vide* Griffith T. Roberts in *Bathafarn*, i. 25–39; and for Howell Harris's supporters in the same district T. J. Hopkins in *J.H.S.P.C.W.* li. 34–44.

[2] Howell Harris spent some time with Wesley at Cardiff, Fonmon, and Wenvoe on 4 Mar., and heard him preach again the following morning. Both men got on well with each other, and on 23 Mar. Harris told George Whitefield that Wesley was 'full of Love and Sweetness and free from all Contentious Spirit'. *J.H.S.P.C.W.*, Supplement 8, 230; *Bathafarn*, vi. 51–3.

TUESDAY, 6. I rode to Fonmon and found Mrs. Jones thoroughly resigned to God although feeling what it was to lose an husband, and such an husband, in the strength of his years.[1]

WEDNESDAY, 7. I returned, and at five in the afternoon preached to a small attentive congregation near Henbury. Before eight I reached Bristol.[2]

VII

3–9 MAY 1743

Bristol · Llangrwyne(?) · Builth · Cardiff · Llantrisant
Fonmon · Cowbridge · Cardiff · Wenvoe · Bristol

TUESDAY, 3 MAY 1743. I set out for Wales [from Bristol], in company with one who was my pupil at Oxford. We could get that night no further than the *Bull*,[3] five Welsh miles beyond Abergavenny. The next morning we came to Builth, just as the church prayers began. Mr. Phillips,[4] the rector of Maesmynys (at whose invitation I came), soon took knowledge of me and we began a friendship which I trust shall never end. I preached on a tomb at the east end of the church at four, and again at seven.[5] Mr. Gwynne and Mr. Protheroe[6] (Justices of the Peace) stood on either hand of me

[1] Robert Jones died on 8 June 1742, aged 36, and was buried in Penmark church. This was obviously a specific visit by Wesley to Fonmon to commiserate with his widow.

[2] Howell Harris was with John Wesley at the society-meeting in Cardiff on 6 July. On the 11th, on his way to Wenvoe church from Aberthaw, he heard how 'dear Mr. [Robert] Jones . . . had desired his Corpse to be encompassed with Methodists'. *Bathafarn*, vi. 58–9.

[3] Possibly a misprint for the Bell, Llangrwyne.

[4] Revd. Edward Phillips (1701–77) retained his Methodist sympathies to the end. *Bathafarn*, xiv. 24–6; xxi. 37; xxiv. 36–7; *J.H.S.P.C.W.* xxxvi. 25; xliii. 23; and *D.W.B.*

[5] Thomas James, the Calvinist exhorter from Crickadarn, states that Wesley 'kept a society' at Builth after preaching twice, and 'prayed with great Power for Brother Harris'. *The Christian History*, iii. 70–1.

[6] Marmaduke Gwynne of Garth (Charles Wesley's father-in-law) and Marmaduke Protheroe of Builth, whose daughter married John Jones, Llanfaredd, a member for a time of the Moravian society at Rhos Goch, Radnorshire, and of their congregation at Leominster. R. T. Jenkins in *Traf. Cym. Hanes Bedyddwyr Cymru*, 1935, 11–13; Robert, *S.T.L.* (*1747–94*), 157 n. 2. For Glwynne, see *J.H.S.P.C.W.* lv. 65–81.

and all the people before, catching every word, with the most serious and eager attention.[1]

THURSDAY, 5. I rode over such rugge dmountains as I never saw before to Cardiff. But it was late before we came in so that I could not preach that night.

FRIDAY, 6. I preached at eleven in the new room which the society had just built in the heart of the town, and our souls were sweetly comforted together.[2] About two, I preached at Llantrisant, and at Fonmon in the evening to a loving and serious congregation.[3]

SATURDAY, 7. I was desired to preach at Cowbridge. We came into the town about eleven, and many people seemed very desirous to hear for themselves concerning the way which is everywhere spoken against. But it could not be. The sons of Belial gathered themselves together, headed by one or two wretches called gentlemen, and continued shouting, cursing, blaspheming and throwing showers of stones, almost without intermission. So that after some time spent in prayer for them, I judged it best to dismiss the congregation.[4]

SUNDAY, 8. I preached in the Castle yard at Cardiff at five in the morning and seven in the evening; in the afternoon at Wenvoe, where the church was quite filled with those who came from many

[1] 'I believe the Lord blessed you much to young Mr. Phillips, the minister, when you were here', wrote Harris to Welsey later in the month; he also mentioned the fact to George Whitefield. Roberts, *S.T.L.* (*1742–47*), 97; *The Christian History*, iii. 82.

[2] This first 'New Room' in Wales was evidently built between Wesley's last visit on 6 July 1742 (when Howell Harris met him in the 'Society House') and 6 May 1743. It stood in Church Street and was enlarged in 1829; this date (1829) is still to be seen above the shops into which it has long been converted.

[3] Howell Griffith of Trefeurig, who was at Wenvoe on 3 Mar. 1743, was told by the curate, the Revd. Philip Thomas, that the society at Fonmon was increasing daily; Thomas had had about 200 hearers there the previous Tuesday night. *The Christian History*, iii. 30–1.

[4] This scene occurred in front of the old Town Hall (now demolished), which stood in the middle of the High Street near the Duke of Wellington inn. L. J. Hopkin-James, *Old Cowbridge*, 53, 203; Jackson, *Journal*, i. 405.

miles round. And God answered many of them in the joy of their hearts. It was a solemn and refreshing season.[1]

MONDAY, 9. I returned to Bristol.

VIII

26 SEPTEMBER–3 OCTOBER 1743

Bristol · Caerleon · Crickhowell · Garth · Cardiff
Fonmon · Cardiff · Caerphilly · Llantrisant · Cardiff · Wenvoe
Porthkerry · Cardiff · Bristol

MONDAY, 26 SEPTEMBER 1743. I had a great desire to speak plain to a young man who went with us over the New Passage. To that end I rode with him three miles out of my way, but I could fix nothing upon him. Just as we parted, walking over Caerleon bridge, he stumbled and was like to fall. I caught him and began to speak of God's care over us. Immediately the tears stood in his eyes and he appeared to feel every word which was said; so I spoke and spared not. The same I did to a poor man who led my horse over the bridge, to our landlord and his wife, and to one who occasionally came in. And they all expressed a surprising thankfulness. About seven in the evening we reached Crickhowell, four miles beyond Abergavenny.

TUESDAY, 27. We came to Mr. Gwynne's at Garth. It brought fresh to my mind our first visit to Mr. Jones at Fonmon. How soon may the master of this great house too be called away into everlasting habitation!

Having so little time to stay I had none to lose. So the same afternoon, about four o'clock, I read prayers and preached to a small congregation on the faith which is *counted to us for righteousness*.

---

[1] Howell Harris was among his hearers at Cardiff. He tells us that Wesley was obliged to preach on the Castle green because of the threat of persecutors to disturb the service if it were held in the New Room. *The Christian History*, iii. 79.

Very early in the morning I was obliged to set out in order to reach Cardiff before it was dark. I found a large congregation waiting there, to whom I explained *Zech.* ix, 11: *By the blood of thy covenant I have sent forth thy prisoners out of the pit wherein is no water.*

THURSDAY, 29. I preached at the castle of Fonmon to a loving, simple people.

FRIDAY, 30. It being a fair, still evening I preached in the Castle yard at Cardiff, and the whole congregation, rich and poor, behaved as in the presence of God.

SATURDAY, 1 OCTOBER. I preached at Caerphilly in the morning, Llantrisant at noon, and Cardiff at night.

SUNDAY, 2. Fearing my strength would not suffice for preaching more than four times in the day, I only spent half an hour in prayer with the society in the morning. At seven, and in the evening, I preached in the Castle, at eleven in Wenvoe church, and in the afternoon in Porthkerry church on *Repent ye and believe the gospel.*

MONDAY, 3. I returned to Bristol.

IX

19–28 APRIL 1744

Minehead · Fonmon · Cardiff · Garth · Maesmynys · Builth Maesmynys · Llan-ddew · Gelli-gaer · Cardiff · Fonmon Bristol

WEDNESDAY, 18 APRIL 1744. Between five and six in the evening we reached Minehead. Finding a general expectation of it among the people, about seven I preached near the sea-shore to almost all the inhabitants of the place. Most of the gentlemen of the town were there and behaved with seriousness and decency.

THURSDAY, 19. Having a sloop ready, which came on purpose,[1] we ran over the Channel in about four hours. Some of our friends were waiting for us on the shore.[2] About one we came to Fonmon Castle. I found a natural wish, 'O for ease and a resting place!'. Not yet. But eternity is at hand! I preached at six, and at five in the morning.

FRIDAY, 20. About ten we set out for Cardiff where, in the evening, I preached in the Castle yard. All were serious and attentive.

SATURDAY, 21. I rode to Garth in Breconshire and on SUNDAY, the 22nd, preached in the church there,[3] both morning and afternoon. On MONDAY, the 23rd, I preached in Maesmynys church and afterwards in the churchyard at Builth.[4] I observed only one man with his hat on, probably through inattention, for he likewise kneeled down on the grass with the rest as soon as I began to pray.

TUESDAY, 24. I preached at Maesmynys again, and about five in Llan-ddew church[5] near Brecon. Such a church I never saw before. There was not a glass window belonging to it but only boards, with holes bored here and there, through which a dim light glimmered in. Yet even here may the light of God's countenance shine. And it shone on many hearts.

---

[1] The sloop probably belonged to the brother of Mrs. Robert Jones, Fonmon. Cf. *post*, p. 21 n. 3.

[2] At Ffontygari or Aberthaw.

[3] Llanlleonfel church. The living belonged to the Prebendary of Llanwrthwl in the Collegiate Church of Brecon. In 1744 Joshua Thomas, a native of the parish and vicar of nearby Merthyr Cynog, served it as curate. *N.L.W. Journal*, xvi. 269–70.

[4] The incumbent of St. Mary's church, Builth, from 1730 to 1768 was the Revd. Thomas Davies. It is safe to assume that he was opposed to Methodism, for not once did Wesley preach inside his church. Edward Phillips, on the other hand, freely gave him the use of his church at Maesmynys; incidentally, he lived at Builth, not at Maesmynys.

[5] The incumbent of Llan-ddew from 1741 to 1783 was Thomas Lewis; he was also licensed to the curacy of Talach-ddu on 26 Aug. 1759. He was the son of the Revd. David Lewis, the evangelical clergyman of Llanfihangel Cwm Deuddwr, Rhaeadr. The son, like the father, sympathized with Methodism, and according to Richard Bennett this cost him his curacy at Merthyr Cynog. He worked very closely with the Welsh Methodists in the early years. *Brycheiniog*, ii. 69 n. 6; Bennett, *Blynyddoedd Cyntaf Methodistiaeth*, 156–7; Jones, *History of Breconshire*, 244; *J.H.S.P.C.W.* xxxviii. 43–4; Roberts, *S.T.L.* (*1742–47*)—see Index, but especially pp. 56, 72, 80.

WEDNESDAY, 25. We rode over the still snowy mountains. At twelve I preached at Gelli-gaer,[1] in the evening at Cardiff, and the next evening at Fonmon. On SATURDAY, the 28th, I returned to Bristol.

X

19–25 JULY 1745

Minehead · Fonmon · Cardiff · Wenvoe · Cardiff · Garth
Maesmynys · Builth · Maesmynys · Llan-ddew · Bristol

WEDNESDAY, 17 JULY 1745. I rode to Mr. Thompson's[2] near Barnstaple and the next evening to Minehead. Early on FRIDAY, the 19th, we went on board[3] and in about four hours crossed the Channel and reached Fonmon.

We were here, as it were, in a new world, in peace, honour and abundance. How soon should I melt away in this sunshine! But the goodness of God suffered it not. In the morning I rode to Cardiff, where also there had been much disturbance, but now all was

[1] Probably at the invitation of the curate, the Revd. Philip Thomas, who wholeheartedly supported Methodism, much to the displeasure of the incumbent, the Revd. Gregory Perrott. Thomas left Gelligaer at an unknown date to become curate to John Hodges at Wenvoe and was the means of forming a number of Methodist societies in Glamorgan (*post*, p. 25 n. 1). He seems to have lived at Fonmon Castle (possibly as chaplain to Mrs. Robert Jones), and in 1753 was presented by her to the living of Michaelston-le-Pit (with the curacy of Sully) and remained there until his death in 1781, aged 71. *J.H.S.P.C.W.* xvi. 157; li. 40–2; Jackson, *Journal*, i. 257; *Bathafarn*, iv. 58; Roberts, *S.T.L. (1742–74)*, 54; C. Tylney, *History of the Parishes of St. Andrew Major and Michaelston-le-Pit*, 52–3; *The Christian History*, iii. 30–1; and Telford, *Letters*, ii. 128—where John Wesley in Feb. 1748 was sorry to hear that he was thinking 'of leaving Mr. Hodges'.

[2] The Revd. George Thompson, rector of St. Gennys, Cornwall. Wesley had just spent five weeks in Cornwall where he and some of his followers had suffered much persecution.

[3] Mrs. Robert Jones, Fonmon, before her marriage in 1732 was Mary Forrest, fifth daughter of Robert Forrest of Minehead and Aberthaw. The sloop belonged to her brother. On 18 June Wesley had written to her: 'On Thursday July 18 . . . Mr. Thompson will come with me to Minehead, from whence, if your brother's sloop was ready, we could cross over to Fonmon.' He added that he had also notified John Hodges of Wenvoe of his plans, so that he could so arrange his affairs as to be able to accompany him to Garth and thence to the annual Conference at Bristol. *Wesley Letters*: 4, printed in Telford, *Letters*, ii. 36–7.

calm. I preached there in the evening. God gave a blessing with His word and we greatly rejoiced before Him.

SUNDAY, 21. I preached at Cardiff at five and at Wenvoe morning and afternoon. In the evening I preached again at Cardiff, in the Castle yard, on *Great is the mystery of godliness*. I never saw such a congregation in Wales before, and all behaved as men fearing God.

MONDAY, 22. I preached at half an hour after four and then set out with Mr. Hodges, rector of Wenvoe, for Garth. Mr. Phillips[1] guided us till he thought all the difficulty was over. But it proved otherwise for, almost as soon as he left us, the night coming on, we got out of the road and might very probably have wandered till daylight had not a gentleman met us and rode out of his way to show us to Mr. Gwynne's house.

TUESDAY, 23. I preached about noon at Maesmynys to a larger congregation than the church could contain. About three I preached at Builth. Five clergymen of us were present,[2] two Justices of the Peace,[3] and well-nigh all the grown people in the town. I had not known so solemn a season before since we came into Wales.

WEDNESDAY, 24. I preached at Builth again, and afterwards at Maesmynys. Thence Mr. Phillips rode with us to Llan-ddew church, where I preached at six to a small, serious congregation. And the next evening, THURSDAY the 25th, came back safe, blessed be God, to Bristol.

---

[1] Edward Phillips, Maesmynys. The following month (3 Sept.) he and Marmaduke Gwynne visited Fonmon in order to take Charles Wesley to Garth, but they were obliged to return without him because of a swollen foot, made worse by the use of 'British oil'—but probably 'the counterfeit sort'! Jackson, *Journal*, i. 403.

[2] Probably Edward Phillips, Maesmynys; Thomas Lewis, Llan-ddew; Rice Williams, Llansanffraid-yn-Elfael; John Hodges; and Wesley himself.

[3] No doubt Marmaduke Gwynne and Marmaduke Protheroe. Gwynne returned with Wesley to Bristol and (like Hodges) attended the Conference. On 31 July he accompanied John and Charles Wesley to examine the society at Bristol. *Min. of Conf.* i. 6; Jackson, *Journal*, i. 401.

PLATE 2

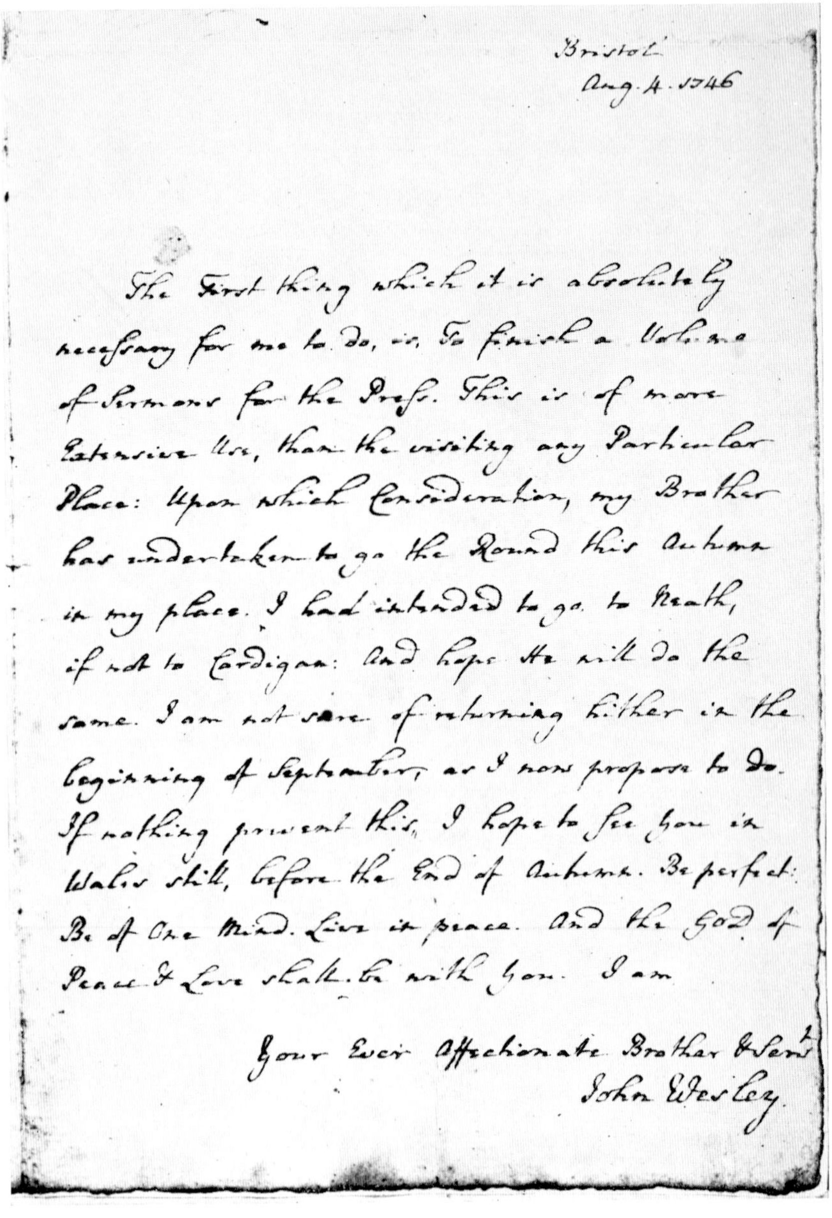

Bristol
Aug. 4. 1746

The First thing which it is absolutely necessary for me to do, is, To finish a Volume of Sermons for the Press. This is of more Extensive Use, than the visiting any Particular Place: Upon which Consideration, my Brother has undertaken to go the Round this Autumn in my place. I had intended to go to Neath, if not to Cardigan: And hope He will do the same. I am not sure of returning hither in the beginning of September, as I now propose to do. If nothing prevent this, I hope to see You in Wales still, before the End of Autumn. Be perfect: Be of One Mind. Live in peace. And the God of Peace & Love shall be with You. I am

Your Ever Affectionate Brother & Serv[t]
John Wesley

Letter from John Wesley to Mary Jones, Fonmon

XI

11–23 AUGUST 1746

Bristol · Abergavenny · Maesmynys · Builth
Llansanffraid-yn-Elfael · Builth · Leominster · Maesmynys
Merthyr Cynog · Cardiff · Wenvoe · Cardiff · Neath
Margam · Bridgend · Fonmon · Wilton · Llan-maes · Bristol

SUNDAY, 10 AUGUST, 1746. In the evening, having determined to spend a little time in Wales,[1] I rode to Sister Crocker's[2] to be ready for the passage in the morning. On MONDAY the 11th, we came to the water-side at half an hour after five, but we did not pass till near twelve, and then rode on to Abergavenny. Mr. Phillips[3] afterwards met us on the road and brought us to a friend's house between nine and ten.

TUESDAY, 12. I preached at Maesmynys church, and in the afternoon in Builth churchyard. The greatest part of the town was present there as usual, and God gave us the usual blessing.

WEDNESDAY, 13. I preached at Llansanffraid.[4] As soon as we came out of the church a poor woman met us whom Satan had bound in an uncommon manner for several years. She followed us to the house where our horses were, weeping and rejoicing and praising God. Two clergymen were there besides me,[5] and the

---

[1] On this journey Wesley had originally intended going as far as Carmarthen and Cardigan (Telford, *Letters*, ii. 79). The unexpected detour to Leominster on 14 Aug. upset his plans, and in the event he did not visit Carmarthen until 1763 and Cardigan until 1777.

[2] Sister Crocker was a Methodist who lived near the Old Passage. Curnock, iii. 250 n. 2.

[3] Edward Phillips, Maesmynys once again.

[4] Wesley preached three times in Llansanffraid-yn-Elfael church between 1746 and 1748, but on each occasion he omitted to mention the name of the incumbent. He was the Revd. Rice Williams, a native of Llangadog, who was appointed curate of Llangyfelach in 1727 and collated to the living of Llansanffraid in 1733, where he remained until his death in 1784 in his 80th year; at an unknown date he was made a Prebendary in the Collegiate Church of Christ, Brecon. He welcomed both John and Charles Wesley to his church, and was equally sympathetic to the Welsh Methodists. *Bathafarn*, xxi. 35–6; *J.H.S.P.C.W.* li. 28.

[5] Probably Rice Williams and Edward Phillips.

house was full of people, but she could not refrain from declaring before them all what God had done for her soul. And the words which came from the heart went to the heart. I scarce ever heard such a preacher before. All were in tears round about her, high and low, for there was no resisting the Spirit by which she spoke.

The odd account she gave of herself was this (concerning which let everyone judge as he pleases): That near seven years since she affronted one of her neighbours, who thereupon went to Francis Morgan (a man famous in those parts) and gave him fourteen shillings to do his worst to her; that the next night, as soon as she was in bed, there was a sudden storm of thunder, lightning and rain, in the midst of which she felt all her flesh shudder and knew the devil was close to her; that at the same time a horse she had in the stable below, which used to be as quiet as a lamb, leaped to and fro and tore in such a manner that she was forced to rise and turn him out; that a tree which grew at the end of the house was torn up by the roots; that from henceforth she had no rest day or night, being not only in fear and horror of mind but in the utmost torment of body, feeling as if her flesh was tearing off with burning pincers; that till this day she had never had any respite or ease; but now she knew God had delivered her, and she believed He would still deliver her body and soul and bruise Satan under her feet.

At three in the afternoon I preached at Builth, designing to go from thence to Carmarthen. But notice having been given, by a mistake, of my preaching at Leominster in Herefordshire, I altered my design and going to Llansanffraid that night, the next day rode to Leominster. . . .

FRIDAY, 15. At four we had another kind of congregation at Maesmynys;[1] many who had drank largely of the grace of God. I examined them, *Do ye now believe*? And the word was as a two-edged sword. After taking sweet leave of this loving people, we rode with honest John Price of Merthyr to his house.[2] We had four

---

[1] Different from the one at Kington earlier in the day: 'One half stood near, the other part remained a little way off and louered defiance. But the Bridle from above was in their mouth so that they made no disturbance at all.'

[2] A Welsh Calvinistic Methodist exhorter who lived at Merthyr Cynog in Breconshire.

hours rain in the morning but a fair, mild afternoon, in the close of which we came to Cardiff.

SUNDAY, 17. I preached at Wenvoe church, morning and afternoon; at five in the evening in the Castle yard at Cardiff, to the far largest congregation which I had ever seen in Wales. All stood uncovered and attentive and, I trust, few went empty away.

MONDAY, 18. I rode with Mr. Hodges to Neath.[1] Here I found twelve young men whom I could almost envy. They lived together in one house and continually gave away whatever they earned above the necessaries of life. Most of them (they told me) were Predestinarians, but so little bigoted to their opinion that they would not suffer a Predestinarian to preach among them unless he would lay all controversy aside. And on these terms they gladly received those of the opposite opinion.

The multitude of people obliged me to preach in the street on *Repent ye and believe the gospel*. One man would fain have interrupted and had procured a druken fiddler for his second. But finding none to join them they were ashamed, so the gentleman stole away on one side and the fiddler on the other.

TUESDAY, 19. I preached again at five. Whatever prejudice remained now vanished away as a dream, and our souls took acquaintance with each other as having all drank into one spirit.[2]

About ten I preached in my return at Margam on *By grace are ye saved through faith*. There being many present who did not well understand English, one repeated to them in Welsh the substance of what I had said. At one we came to Bridgend, where I preached on a small green not far from the church[3] on *Jesus Christ, made of*

---

[1] In Dec. 1746 Hodges's curate, Philip Thomas, invited William Holland to accompany him on a visit to his societies—and he was at pains to emphasize that they *were* his societies, not Wesley's, Harris's, Whitefield's or anyone else's. Holland agreed, and the two men visited Llan-maes, Margam, and Neath. It was surely no coincidence that Hodges took Wesley to these same three places. *J.H.S.P.C.W.* xvii. 6–8.

[2] This, Wesley's first visit to Neath, evidently gave Howell Harris some concern, for it was discussed at the Association at Bristol the following January, *ante*, pp. xxviii–xxix.

[3] Probably Oldcastle (or, more accurately, St. Mary's church, Nolton), a chapel of ease to Coety, *post*, p. 88.

God unto us wisdom, righteousness, sanctification and redemption.
It being the time of the yearly revel, we had many strangers from all
parts, but none behaved unseemly; none opened his mouth; for
the fear of God was amongst them. In the evening I preached at
Fonmon Castle on the fruits of the Spirit. I concluded the day with
the little society there, rejoicing and praising God.

WEDNESDAY, 20. I preached near Wilton, a little town about
a mile from Cowbridge,¹ and on THURSDAY at Llan-maes,
four miles from Fonmon to a people of simple, loving, childlike
spirit.

FRIDAY, 22. I returned to Cardiff and spoke plain to those who
were wise in their own eyes. This however was matter of joy: they
were willing to receive reproof, otherwise I should have feared
that with regard to them I had laboured in vain.

SATURDAY, 23. Returning to Bristol, I found poor C.G. there
proclaiming open war. . . .

XII

4–8 AUGUST 1747

*Bristol · Builth · Caernarfon · Moel y don · Llangefni
Holyhead · Dublin*

TUESDAY, 4 AUGUST 1747. I set out for Ireland² [from
Bristol]. We rode that day (but it was hard labour) to Builth,
where I preached in the evening on the Prodigal Son.

WEDNESDAY, 5. Taking horse early in the morning, we rode
over the rough mountains of Radnorshire and Montgomeryshire

---

¹ So far from being 'a little town', Wilton is a farm some 3 miles south-west of
Cowbridge. The nearest township is Siginston and Wesley may have preached there
and stayed overnight at Wilton.
² Wesley on this, his first journey through Wales to Ireland, was accompanied by
two of his Preachers, William Tucker and John Trembath.

into Merioneth. In the evening I was surprised with one of the finest prospects in its kind that ever I saw in my life. We rode in a green vale, shaded with rows of trees, which made an arbour for several miles. The river laboured along on our right hand through broken rocks of every size, shape and colour. On the other side of the river the mountain rose to an immense height, almost perpendicular; and yet the tall, straight oaks stood, rank above rank, from the bottom to the very top; only here and there, where the mountain was not so steep, were interposed pastures or fields of corn. At a distance, as far as the eye could reach, as it were by way of contrast:

> A mountain huge upreared
> Its broad, bare back. . . .

with vast, rugged rocks hanging over its brow, that seemed to nod portending ruin.[1]

THURSDAY, 6. Between three and four in the afternoon we with some difficulty reached Caernarfon.[2] This has the face of a fortified town, having walls (such as they are) and a castle as considerable as that of Cardiff. Here we parted with our guide and interpreter, Mr. Phillips. Mr. Tucker and I set out for Holyhead. We intended to cross over into Anglesey at Moel y don ferry,[3] four miles from Caernarfon, but not being able to inquire our way (as we spoke no Welsh and the country people no English) we could not find where the ferry was till we saw the boat coming over. We went into the boat about sunset, and lodged that night at a little inn by the waterside.

FRIDAY, 7. We made a little stop at Llangefni, seven miles from the ferry. We should have hired a guide to have steered over the sands, but it was quite out of my mind till we came to them; so we

[1] The reference in this paragraph is to the Dyfi Valley, with Cader Idris in the background.

[2] Roads in Montgomeryshire were not improved until the Montgomeryshire Turnpike Trust was formed in 1769, those in Merioneth not until 1775, and the road from Pwllheli to Caernarfon until 1777. A. H. Dodd, *The Industrial Revolution in North Wales*, 92 and in *Arch. Camb.*, 1925, 137.

[3] The present village of Port Dinorwic stands on the Caernarvonshire side of the ferry.

went straight across and came to Holyhead without any stop or hindrance at all.[1]

SATURDAY, 8. Finding one of the packet-boats ready, we went aboard about eight o'clock in the morning. It was a dead calm when we rowed out of the harbour. But about two in the afternoon the wind sprung up and continued till near four on Sunday morning, when we were within sight of the Irish shore.

I could not but observe: 1. that while we were sailing with a fresh gale there was no wind at all a mile off, but a ship which lay ahead of us was quite becalmed, till we left her out of sight. 2. that a French privateer, which for several days had taken every ship which sailed on that coast, was taken and brought into Dublin bay the very morning we arrived there.

Before ten we came to St. George's quay. . . .[2]

XIII

26 AUGUST–5 SEPTEMBER 1747

*Dublin · Holyhead · Rhyd-sbardun · Caernarfon · Tan-y-bwlch
Llanidloes · Builth · Garth · Builth · Maesmynys
Llansanffraid · Clyro · Crickhowell · Risca · Cardiff
Fonmon · Bristol*

SUNDAY, 23 AUGUST 1747. . . . I had then delivered my message. So before ten we took boat [at Dublin] and about eleven

[1] There were no decent roads in Anglesey at this time—merely numerous winding lanes—and those which linked Holyhead to the present site of the Menai Suspension Bridge (through Bodedern and Llangefni) were not converted into a turnpike road until 1765. There were not even milestones on the island before 1752, and when they appeared, they were provided by the owner of the Dublin packet. A. H. Dodd, *Arch. Camb.*, 1925, 130, 132. The present A. 5 (which replaced the old Holyhead road) was not constructed until 1823. Before the construction of the embankment which connects Holy Island with the mainland (our A. 5), travellers were obliged to cross the narrow neck of water by boat or walk over the sands when the tide was out.

[2] Wesley does not appear to have preached at all in Anglesey on this journey—not even at Holyhead, where he stayed overnight. But William Morris informed his brother Richard (who was in London) that he had 'dispersed his sermons' and that it was fortunate for him that the vicar, the Revd. Thomas Ellis, was not at home, 'else there would have been a scuffle'. Quoted by R. T. Jenkins in *Bathafarn*, ii. 50.

reached the ship. The wind was right ahead. Then succeeded a dead calm, so that we did not get out of the bay till MONDAY evening nor within sight of Wales till WEDNESDAY the 26th. By this means we had an opportunity of talking largely both with our fellow-passengers and the sailors, many of whom received our words with gladness. About two in the afternoon we landed at Holyhead. Between three and four we took horse and came in the evening to Thomas Thomas', near Rhyd-sbardun.[1] He had before desired Jonathan Reeves[2] to call there in his return. But we were at a great loss, none in the house understanding English and none of us understanding Welsh; till Mr. Morgan,[3] a neighbouring school-master, came who took us to his own house, and in the morning, THURSDAY the 27th, rode with us to the passage. We reached Caernarfon before ten, Tan-y-bwlch in the evening, and Llanidloes FRIDAY the 28th.

SATURDAY, 29. About noon we came to Builth. At three I preached in the main street and at Garth in the evening, where I met my brother, going to Ireland.[4]

SUNDAY, 30. He preached at Builth about nine. Thence we went to Maesmynys church, but it would not near contain the congregation, so that I was constrained to preach in the churchyard. Thence I rode to Llansanffraid. Here also the church not being able to hold the people, I came out to a large tombstone under a shady tree and proclaimed *the grace of our Lord Jesus Christ*. One of the audience

---

[1] One of the three sons of the Dissenter Thomas Prichard, who lived at Pen-yr-allt, Cerrig Ceinwen. Dafydd Wyn Wiliam in *Y Cofiadur*, xxxvi. 48.

[2] One of Wesley's Preachers, who eventually became a clergyman.

[3] Jenkin Morgan (d. 1762). A native of South Wales, he 'conducted' schools for the Revd. Griffith Jones, Llanddowror at various places, including Glasfryn Fawr, the home of William Prichard (later of Clwchdernog), before moving to Anglesey in 1742 (*ante*, p. xxv). After his marriage in July 1746 he probably lived at Trehwfa Bach, Cerrig Ceinwen, until he bought Tŷ'n-yr-aethnen (in the parish of Llangefni) in 1759. Dafydd Wyn Wiliam, op. cit. 41–67, which supplements *J.H.S.P.C.W.* xxxviii. 37 and *D.W.B.*, s.n.

[4] Charles Wesley and Charles Perronet were staying with Edward Phillips at Builth awaiting the arrival of brother John. While they were there, Marmaduke Gwynne and two of his family arrived. 'My soul', wrote Charles afterwards, 'seemed pleased to take acquaintance with them.' (Jackson, *Journal*, i. 454.) In less than two years Charles married Marmaduke's daughter Sally.

pressed me much to preach at Clyro, telling me Mr. J. had often said 'I should be welcome to his pulpit'.

MONDAY, 31. I rode thither and called on Mr. J. but (as I supposed it would) his heart failed.[1] I preached on a large smooth meadow, *Christ our wisdom, righteousness, sanctification and redemption.* And a multitude of people were gathered from all parts, though on so short a warning.

We set out early SEPTEMBER 1, and after a short stop near Crickhowell aimed at the nearest way over the mountains to Cardiff. But it was near four in the afternoon before we could reach a little village at the foot of the hills called Risca. The people at the inn here were civil above measure, particularly a young genteel man who was son to the woman of the house, and lived at a small distance from it. He rode with us two miles to show us the nearest way and desired, if we came again, we would lodge at his house. The reason of all this kindness was that, a year or two ago, he had heard me preach at Bristol.

I reached Cardiff between seven and eight and immediately went to the Room. My strength just lasted till I had done preaching. I was then quite ready to lie down and rest.

WEDNESDAY, 2 SEPTEMBER. I spent some time with T. Prosser who had filled the society with vain janglings.[2] I found the fault lay in his head rather than in his heart. He is an honest, well-meaning man, but no more qualified either by nature or grace to expound Scripture than to read lectures in logic or algebra. Yet even men of sense have taken this dull, mystical man to be far deeper than he is. And it is very natural so to do. If we look into a dark pit it seems deep, but the darkness only makes it seem so. Bring the light and we shall see it is very shallow.

[1] The vicar of Clyro was the Revd. William James. On 11 Nov. 1744 Howell Harris had attended a service there, and had been 'fed and strengthened'—despite 'ye Minister being a fighter, swearing, drunkard and opposer'. There was a Calvinistic Methodist society at Cefn-y-fedwast near by. *J.H.S.P.C.W.* xxxvi. 55–6; xxxviii. 11.

[2] Thomas Prosser (*ante*, pp. xx; xxviii) is by no means an uncommon name, and yet one wonders, in view of the complaints about Prosser's activities among the Calvinists of Breconshire, whether he and the Thomas Prosser who was a member of the Merthyr Cynog society in 1743 were the same person. *J.H.S.P.C.W.* li. 65.

In the evening I preached at Fonmon. But the congregation being larger than the chapel[1] would contain, I was obliged to preach in the court. I was myself much comforted in comforting the weary and heavy-laden.

FRIDAY, 4. There was a very large congregation at Cardiff Castle yard in the evening. I afterwards met the society, spoke plain to them, and left them once more in peace.

SATURDAY, 5. In my road to Bristol I read over Q. Curtius,[2] a fine writer both as to thought and language. . . .

XIV

16 FEBRUARY–8 MARCH 1748

Bristol · Old Passage · Chepstow · Abergavenny · Brecon
Builth · Garth · Llansanffraid · Builth · Garth · Llanidloes
Machynlleth · Tan-y-bwlch · Caernarfon · Holyhead
Llangefni · Llanddaniel · Rhyd-sbardun · Trefollwyn
Llanfihangel Tre'r-beirdd · Glan-y-gors · Holyhead · Dublin

MONDAY, 15 FEBRUARY 1748. I set out for Ireland. We[3] came to the New Passage at ten. After waiting about five hours we found (which they did not dare to confess) that the boatmen did not dare to venture out. It blew a storm. We then rode to the Old Passage but the boat was just gone off.

TUESDAY, 16. They talked of passing early, but the storm was too high. I then walked to Aust where I preached about ten to a

---

[1] Charles Wesley tells us that the dining room at Fonmon was used as a chapel. Jackson, *Journal*, i. 294.

[2] Quintus Curtius, a rhetorician and historian who wrote a history of Alexander the Great in ten books. Wrote under Emperor Claudius (10 B.C.–A.D. 54). *The Oxford Classical Dictionary*, p. 782.

[3] Wesley was accompanied by Robert Swindells (one of his Preachers) and the Revd. John Meriton, a clergyman from the Isle of Man. On 12 Feb. he had explained to Mrs. Robert Jones, Fonmon, that he was obliged to take the shortest route to Holyhead, 'my brother being almost impatient of my arrival'. *Wesley Letters*: 6, printed in Telford, *Letters*, ii. 128.

small, serious congregation. Between four and five, the wind somewhat abating, a boat ventured out and carried us over. We passed
through Chepstow soon after sunset and pushed on, though it
grew dark and the untracked snow lay thick upon the ground.
About eight we reached the *Star*,[1] a good though small inn, five
long miles from Chepstow.

It snowed all night. On WEDNESDAY, 17 we set out before
day but found it bad travelling, there being no path to be seen,
neither footstep of man or beast. However in four or five hours we
reached Abergavenny, and Brecon before three in the afternoon.

Our landlady here almost forced us to take a guide. And it was
extremely well she did, for the snow had so entirely covered the
roads that our guide himself mistook the way more than once. So
that if he had not been with us we should, without doubt, have
lodged upon the mountains.

I preached in the evening at Builth and at noon the next day,
at Garth in the evening and twice on Friday.

SATURDAY, 20. I preached in Maesmynys church in the afternoon, at Garth morning and evening.

SUNDAY, 21. I preached in the morning in Llansanffraid church.
The service at Builth was not over till past two. I then began in the
churchyard, notwithstanding the north-east wind, to call sinners to
repentance. More than all the town was gathered together in that
pleasant vale and made the woods and mountains echo while they
sang:

> Ye mountains and vales in praises abound,
> Ye hills and ye dales, continue the sound;
> Break forth into singing ye trees of the wood,
> For Jesus is bringing lost sinners to God.

In the evening I preached again at Garth, and on MONDAY the
22nd at five in the morning. A little before sunrise we took horse,
it being a clear sharp frost. We had waited four days in hopes the

---

[1] The Star Inn stood (and still stands) about 3 miles north-west of Devauden and
1 mile east of Llansoy. [O.S. grid reference: ST 4502]. Wesley and his companions had
covered about 8 miles through the snow that evening from Chepstow.

snow would melt, fearing the drifts of it would lie deep upon the mountains, particularly as we journeyed northwards. But, quite contrary to our expectations, the farther northward we went the less snow we found, so that it scarce hindered us after the first day. About eleven we came to Llanidloes. At the earnest request of one who lived there, I preached at noon in the market-place[1] to such a congregation as no one could expect at an hour's warning.

It was as much as we could do to reach Machynlleth that night. It snowed again from about midnight till morning, so that no path was to be seen for several miles. However we found our way to Tan-y-bwlch and passed the sands[2] in the afternoon, being determined to reach Caernarfon if possible. And so we did, notwithstanding my horse's losing a shoe, but not till between nine and ten at night.

WEDNESDAY, 24. We hastened on to Holyhead, but all the ships were on the other side.

THURSDAY, 25. No packet-boat being come, I gave notice of preaching in the evening. The hearers were many more than the room would contain and they all behaved with decency.

FRIDAY, 26. I preached again in the evening. Mr. E.,[3] the minister, came in towards the close. He was speaking warmly to

[1] Wesley is said to have preached on a stone which stood outside the market-hall in Llanidloes. A commemorative plaque was fixed to this stone and unveiled by the donor, Mr. W. T. Morris of Llanelli, on the occasion of the first meeting of the Historical Society of the Methodist Church in Wales, 24 Oct. 1946.

[2] The sands of Traeth Mawr, later (1808–11) enclosed and reclaimed by W. A. Madocks—who is also interesting Methodistically because he married the granddaughter of Howell Harris's brother Joseph. R. T. Jenkins, *Yng Nghysgod Trefeca*, 147–53; *Gentleman's Magazine*, 1818, 368; *Trans. Caernarvonshire Historical Society*, iv. 67–85.

[3] The Revd. Thomas Ellis (1712–92), a graduate and later a Fellow of Jesus College, Oxford; in 1737 he was appointed by the college to the lecturership of Holyhead. A very conscientious and rather puritanical clergyman, he was an ardent supporter of the Circulating Schools; a corresponding member of the Cymmrodorion Society; a friend of the Morris brothers; a benefactor of the poet Goronwy Owen; and one of the sponsors of the Welsh Bible published by the S.P.C.K. in 1746. In that year he published *Byrr Grynhoad eglur o'r Grefydd Gristianogol . . .* in which he denounced schism (for he always feared that the Methodists would leave the Church); he was equally anxious to dispel the popular belief which associated the Circulating Schools with Methodism and Dissent. His initial reaction to the landlord, Robert Griffith, therefore, followed

our landlord when Mr. Swindells went to him and spoke a few mild words. Mr. E. asked him to step with him to his lodgings, where they had a long and friendly conversation.

SATURDAY, 27. Mr. Swindells informed me that Mr. E. would take it a favour if I could write some little thing 'to advise the Methodists not to leave the Church and not to rail at their ministers'. I sat down immediately and wrote *A Word to a Methodist* which Mr. E. translated into Welsh and printed.[1]

SUNDAY, 28. In the evening I read prayers at our inn[2] and preached to a large and serious audience. I did the same on MONDAY and TUESDAY evening. Perhaps our stay here may not be in vain.

I never knew men make such poor, lame excuses as these captains did for not sailing. It put me in mind of the epigram:

> There are, if rightly I methink
> Five causes why a man should drink

which, with a little alteration, would just suit them:

> There are, unless my memory fail
> Five causes why we should not sail:
> The fog is thick, the wind is high,
> It rains—or may do by-and-by
> Or—any other reason why.

WEDNESDAY, 2 MARCH. Finding no more probability of sailing now than the first day we came to Holyhead, we rode into

by his request to Wesley, were quite consistent. *D.W.B.*, s.n.; Hugh Owen (ed.), *Additional Letters of the Morrises of Anglesey*, Part II, 553.

[1] *A Word to a Methodist* was published in Welsh at Dublin later that year and reprinted in 1751. On 28 Feb. Wesley informed Howell Harris of his meeting Thomas Ellis: 'He commends you much for bringing the Methodists back to the Church; and at his request I have wrote a little thing to the same effect. He will translate it into Welsh, and then I design to print it both in Welsh and English. I will send you some as soon as I can, that you may disperse them when you see occasion. . . .' Telford, *Letters*, ii. 129.

[2] The landlord was Robert Griffith, and Wesley and his Preachers usually stayed with him at Holyhead (*J.H.S.P.C.W.* iv. 99; xv. 149). Thomas Tobias, Lawrence Coughlan, and William Thompson were 'very well entertained' by him in Sept. 1760. *W.H.S. Proc.* xxvii. 30.

the country to see for Mr. William Jones, who had some acquaintance with my brother.[1] We procured a guide to show us the way to his house, but all we learned there was that he was not at home. We lodged at the *Bull's Head*.[2] All the family came up to prayers, and we had a quiet and comfortable night.

THURSDAY, 3. Mr. Holloway, a neighbouring exciseman, invited us to breakfast with him.[3] He once began to run well and now resolved to set out afresh. I trust we were sent to him for good.

His wife bitterly opposed this way till one day, as she was sitting in her house, a flash of lightning killed a cat which sat just by her and struck her to the earth, scorching her flesh in many parts, and yet not at all singeing her clothes. When she came to herself, she could not but acknowledge the loud call of God. But her seriousness did not continue long; her acquaintances soon laughed her out of it. Yet God called her again in dreams and visions of the night. She thought she was standing in the open air when one appeared in the clouds exceeding glorious above the brightness of the sun. She soon after saw a second and then a third. One had a kind of spear in his hand, the second a besom wherewith he was going to sweep the earth, the third an hour-glass as though time was short. This so deeply affected her that she began from that time to seek God with her whole heart.

At noon we went to Mr. Morgan's, where I lodged in August last.[4] About two we met Mr. Jones and Mr. Williams,[5] a clergyman

[1] William Jones (1718–81), of Trefollwyn Blas (*ante*, p. xxv). Charles Wesley may have met him in Anglesey in Sept. 1747 on his way to Ireland. William Griffith, *Methodistiaeth Fore Môn, 1740–51* (and a review of it by Thomas Richards in *Y Traethodydd*, 1956, 142–4) and in *J.H.S.P.C.W.* li. 1–10; Dafydd Wyn Wiliam in *J.H.S.P.C.W.* liv. 2–9.

[2] In Llangefni.

[3] [Walter ?] Holloway, who lived at Glyn Afon, Llangefni (within a stone's throw of Rhos-meirch chapel), was evidently sympathetic to Welsh Calvinistic Methodism. Howell Harris occasionally called on him and he, too, states that his wife had formerly been an 'opposer'. Dafydd Wyn Wiliam, *y Cofiadur*, xxxvi. 51; W. Griffith, *Methodistiaeth Fore Môn*, 70–1.

[4] Trehwfa Bach.

[5] William Jones and the Revd. William Williams, Pantycelyn. At the Lampeter Association of Welsh Calvinistic Methodism on 3 Feb. 1748 it had been resolved that William Williams should spend a month in the counties of Caernarfon, Anglesey, and Montgomery from 22 Feb. *J.H.S.P.C.W.* l, 88. Cf. Gomer M. Roberts, *Y Pêr Ganiedydd*, i. 79. John Hughes, a Dissenter, probably lived at Rhyd-sbardun.

from South Wales, at Rhyd-sbardun. After Mr. Williams had preached in Welsh, I preached in English. Many understood me and felt the power of God.

FRIDAY, 4. We went to Llanddaniel, a mile or two from Moel y don ferry.[1] Here again Mr. W. preached in Welsh and I in English. I was much pleased with this loving, artless people and readily complied with their request of preaching again in the afternoon.

SATURDAY, 5. At two I preached at Rhyd-sbardun to a little earnest company who were ready to devour every word. We spent the evening very agreeably with Mr. Jones at Trefollwyn.

SUNDAY, 6. We went to Llangefni church, though we understood little of what we heard. O what a heavy curse was the Confusion of Tongues! And how grievous are the effects of it! All the birds of the air, all the beasts of the field, understand the language of their own species. Man only is a barbarian to man, unintelligible to his own brethren!

In the afternoon I preached at Llanfihangel, about six miles southwest of Llangefni.[2] I have not seen a people so deeply affected since we came into Anglesey; their cries and tears continued a long time without any intermission. O that we could declare to them in their own tongue the wonderful works of God!

In the evening I preached at Glan-y-gors.[3] When I had done Mr.

---

[1] More specifically, they went to Bodlew in the parish of Llanddaniel-fab, the home of William Prichard, for whom *vide post*, p. 44 n. 3.

[2] There is no Llanfihangel six miles south-west of Llangefni. The choice seems to lie between Llanfihangel Tre'r-beirdd and Llanfihangel Ysgeifiog, and of the two the former is the more likely. To the arguments adduced in its favour by Griffith T. Roberts (*Bathafarn*, iii. 57–9) two others may be suggested. On 18 Nov. 1750 Howell Harris spoke to the society at 'Llanfihangel' after travelling '5 or 8 miles' through Llannerch-y-medd from Glan-y-gors—and Llanfihangel Ysgeifiog is about 10 miles from Glan-y-gors even as the crow flies; nor need he have taken in Llannerch-y-medd. Secondly, it then took him 3 hours to reach Ysgubor-fawr (some 3 miles south-west of Llangefni); would it have taken him so long from Llanfihangel Ysgeifiog, even via Llangefni, and before Malldraeth marsh was drained? *J.H.S.P.C.W.* xxviii. 53–4.

[3] Though there are at least four farms known as Glan-y-gors in Anglesey, this was probably the one situated about a mile from Nantannog and three miles due west of Llannerch-y-medd. Howell Harris preached at 'Glanygorse by Nantanog in Llantrist Psh' on 27 Oct. 1747 and again on 16 July 1749 (*J.H.S.P.C.W.* xxvi. 12; xxxix. 8; *Bathafarn*, iii. 58). Moreover, in 1749 the incumbent of Llantrisant (and

Jones repeated in Welsh (as he likewise did in the afternoon) the substance of what I had said. The next morning we returned to Holyhead and found there all the packet-boats which we had left.

I was determined not to stay another day at an inn, so in the afternoon I took lodging in a private house not a bow-shot distant from the town and removed thither without delay.[1] My congregation this evening was larger than ever, and several of the gentry agreed to come the next. But it was a little too late, for at midnight the wind came fair and before one we sailed out of the harbour.

XV

19–25 MAY 1748

Dublin · Holyhead · Caernarfon · Builth · Garth · Maesmynys Builth · Merthyr Cynog · Cardiff · Fonmon · Wenvoe Cardiff · Bristol

WEDNESDAY, 18 MAY 1748. We took ship [at Dublin]. The wind was small in the afternoon but exceeding high towards night. About eight I laid me down on the quarter-deck. I was soon wet from head to foot but I took no cold at all. About four in the morning we landed at Holyhead, and in the evening reached Caernarfon.

FRIDAY, 20. I rode with Mr. C. Perronet to Machynlleth, and the next day, SATURDAY 21, to Builth. I had no desire to go further and it rained hard, but Mr. Phillips[2] pressed us to go on to Garth. We came thither just as they were singing before family prayer, so I took the book and preached on those words, *Behold, to fear the Lord, that is wisdom and to depart from evil, that is understanding.*

Glan-y-gors and Nantannog were in his parish) reported that there were five families 'in this Rectory' who met 'in a certain place as Methodists'. *J.H.S.P.C.W.* xv. 149. Cf. *Er Clod*, 47.

   [1] Could this have been the home of Owen Dafydd, a cooper and a Methodist exhorter who lived near Holyhead and who held Methodist meetings in his house?

   [2] Edward Phillips, Maesmynys.

SUNDAY, 22. At eight I preached at Garth, afterwards in Maes-mynys church, and at Builth in the afternoon. We proposed going this evening to John Price's at Merthyr,[1] but fearing that he might be at the society (two miles from his house) we went round that way and came while the exhorter was in the midst of his sermon. I preached when he had done. About eight we came to Merthyr[2] and slept in peace.

MONDAY, 23. We were on horseback at four o'clock and at four in the afternoon came to Cardiff. The rain obliged me to preach in the Room.

TUESDAY, 24. I breakfasted at Fonmon, dined at Wenvoe, and preached at Cardiff in the evening.

WEDNESDAY, 25. We set out after preaching and in the after-noon came to Bristol.

XVI

17–22 FEBRUARY 1749

Ross · Garth · Maesmynys · Builth · Garth · Raglan · Bristol

THURSDAY, 16 FEBRUARY 1749. We rode to Ross, and on FRIDAY to Garth.[2]

---

[1] i.e. Merthyr Cynog in Breconshire, not Merthyr Tydfil in Glamorgan (as implied by Curnock, iii. 354 n. 3).

[2] This visit was made specifically in connection with Charles Wesley's forthcoming marriage to Sally Gwynne. The two brothers were accompanied by Charles Perronet, the son of the Revd. Vincent Perronet, vicar of Shoreham. It was agreed that John should give his brother security for the payment of £100 per annum out of the profits of their publications, and that Marmaduke Gwynne and Vincent Perronet should act as trustees of the property secured to Charles Wesley and his bride. Charles Perronet left Garth with John Wesley on the 21st, but Charles stayed on until the 27th. During his stay, Sally Gwynne promised to allow him to itinerate after their marriage—and to continue with his vegetarian diet. Jackson, *Journal*, ii. 52; *Life*, i. 521; Tyerman, *Wesley*, ii. 34.

PLATE 3

Pulpit said to have been used by John Wesley at Bedwas
By permission of the National Museum of Wales, Welsh Folk Museum

SUNDAY, 19. My brother preached at Maesmynys in the morning. I preached at Builth in the afternoon, and at Garth in the evening.

TUESDAY, 21. I rode to Raglan, and the next day to Kingswood.

XVII

3–15 APRIL 1749

Bristol · New Passage · Bedwas · Cardiff · Llan-maes · Fonmon
Cowbridge · Llantrisant · Aberdare · Garth · Builth
Maesmynys · Garth · Llanidloes · Dinas Mawddwy · Dolgellau
Tan-y-bwlch · Caernarfon · Holyhead · Dunleary

MONDAY, 3 APRIL 1749. I set out for Ireland. We waited more than four hours at the Passage, by which delay I was forced to disappoint a large congregation at Newport.[1] About three I came to Bedwas near Caerphilly.[2] The congregation had waited some hours. I began immediately, wet and weary as I was, and we rejoiced over all our labours.

In the evening and the next morning (TUESDAY the 4th) I preached at Cardiff. O what a fair prospect was here some years ago! Surely this whole town would have known God, from the least to the greatest, had it not been for men leaning to their own understanding instead of *the Law and the Testimony*.[3]

At twelve I preached at Llan-maes to a loving, earnest people who do not desire to be any wiser than God. In the evening I preached at Fonmon,[4] the next morning at Cowbridge. How is the

---

[1] Charles Wesley, who was with him, tells us that 'brother Thomas' met them on the Welsh side of the Severn—probably the father of John Thomas, Newport.

[2] There were Arminian societies by this time at Bedwas, Cardiff, Llanwynno, and Llantrisant, for on 8 Apr. Thomas William, the Calvinist exhorter from Eglwysilan, informed Howell Harris that John Wesley had visited 'his societies' there 'last week' (*J.H.S.P.C.W.* xxx. 30). The preaching-desk (Plate 3) which Wesley is said to have used at Pant Glas, Bedwas is now at the Welsh Folk Museum, St. Fagans.

[3] Doubtless a reference to Thomas Prosser's disruptive influence.

[4] John Hodges met them at Fonmon. He did not approve of Charles's marriage. Jackson, *Journal*, ii. 54.

scene changed since I was here last, amidst the madness of the people and the stones flying on every side! Now all is calm; the whole town is in good humour and flock to hear the glad tidings of salvation. In the evening I preached at Llantrisant.

THURSDAY, 6. We rode to a hard-named place on the top of a mountain.[1] I scarce saw any house near. However, a large number of honest, simple people soon came together; few could understand me so Henry Lloyd, when I had done, repeated the substance of my sermon in Welsh.[2] The behaviour of the people recompensed us for our labour in climbing up to them.

About noon we came to Aberdare, just as the bell was ringing for a burial. This had brought a great number together, to whom, after the burial, I preached in the church.[3] We had almost continued rains from Aberdare to the great rough mountain that hangs over the vale of Brecon, but as soon as we gained the top of this we left the clouds behind us. We had a mild, fair, sunshiny evening the remainder of our journey.[4]

FRIDAY, 7. We reached Garth.

SATURDAY, 8. I married my brother and Sarah Gwynne. It was a solemn day, such as became the dignity of a Christian marriage.[5]

[1] Llanwynno fits this description very well, especially as Thomas William mentions it as one of the places (and societies) visited by Wesley on this journey. From Charles Wesley's *Journal* we learn that the two brothers stayed overnight at Llantrisant and that John preached at 5 a.m., at 9 (presumably at Llanwynno), and at 12 (at Aberdare). Op. cit. ii. 54.

[2] Henry Lloyd of Rhydri, Glamorgan. A Welsh-speaking Welshman, he was one of Wesley's Itinerant Preachers for a short while but later spent the greater part of his life as a local preacher. He was on good terms with the Welsh Calvinists and wrote elegies on Howell Harris and George Whitefield. *Bathafarn*, xxiv. 38 and the references therein.

[3] The church of St. John the Baptist, a chapelry of Llantrisant, of which Richard Harris was vicar.

[4] The two brothers reached Brecon by 7 p.m. and stayed there overnight. During the evening Charles, accompanied by Thomas James, a Brecon attorney, obtained a fiat for his marriage from the Surrogate, the Revd. Edward Williams, vicar of Llansbyddyd. Jackson, op. cit. ii. 54.

[5] Charles fills in the details: 'Not a cloud was to be seen from morning till night. I rose at four; spent three hours and a half in prayer or singing with my brother, with

SUNDAY, 9. I preached at Builth, Maesmynys and Garth.

MONDAY, 10. A little after ten we reached Llanidloes. Many were come thither before us from all parts. About eleven I preached in the market-place. The wind was so piercing that whenever it came in my face it almost took away my voice. But the poor people (though all of them stood bareheaded) seemed not to know there was any wind at all. We rode from hence in three hours to a village seven miles off.[1] The persons at whose house we called, knowing who we were, received us with open arms and gladly gave us such fare as they had. In three hours more we rode with much ado seven miles farther to a village named Dinas Mawddwy. Here an honest man, out of pure goodwill, without my knowing anything of the matter, sent for the most learned man in the town, who was an exciseman, to bear me company. He sent an excuse, being not very well, but withal invited me to his house. I returned him thanks and sent him two or three little books, on which he wrote a few lines, begging me to call upon him. I went, and found one that wanted a Saviour and was deeply sensible of his want. I spent some time with him in conversation and prayer, and had reason to hope the seed was sown in good ground.

TUESDAY, 11. We reached Dolgellau in less than three hours, Tan-y-bwlch before noon and Caernarfon in the evening. What need there is of guides over these sands I cannot conceive. This is the third time I have crossed them without any.

WEDNESDAY, 12. We came to Holyhead between one and two, but all the ships were on the Irish side. One came in the next day

---

Sally, with Beck. At eight I led my Sally to church [Llanlleonfel]. Her father, sisters, Lady Rudd, Grace Bowen, Betty Williams and, I think, Billy Tucker and Mr. James were all the persons present. . . . We walked back to the house and joined again in prayer. Prayer and thanksgiving was our whole employment. We were cheerful without mirth, serious without sadness. A stranger, that intermeddleth not with our joy, said "It looked more like a funeral than a wedding". My brother seemed the happiest person among us.' Jackson, op. cit. ii. 55–6.

[1] John Wesley continued on his way with William ('Billy') Tucker, one of his Preachers, at 4 a.m. It is impossible to identify the village at which they stayed; no village stands 7 miles from Llanidloes and another 7 from Dinas Mawddwy. Wesley's estimate of the miles he covered on this occasion may have been wide of the mark, and this particular village may have been Cemaes.

but could not go out, the wind being quite contrary. In this journey I read over Statius' *Thebais*.[1] I wonder one man should write so well and so ill. Sometimes he is scarce inferior to Virgil, sometimes as low as the dullest parts of Ovid.

In the evening I preached on *Be ye also ready*. The poor people now seemed to be much affected, and equally so the next night, so that I was not sorry the wind was contrary.

SATURDAY, 15. We went on board at six, the wind then standing due east, but no sooner were we out of harbour than it turned south-west and blew a storm. . . . But in the night we got back into Dublin bay and landed soon after three at Dunleary, about seven English miles from the city.

XVIII

19 MARCH–7 APRIL 1750

Bristol · New Passage · Cardiff · Aberdare · Brecon · Builth
Rhaeadr · Llanidloes · Machynlleth · Dolgellau · Tan-y-bwlch
Moel y don · Rhos-meirch · Trefollwyn · Clwchdernog
Llangefni · Llannerch-y-medd · Llangefni · Llannerch-y-medd
Trefollwyn · Holyhead · Dublin

SUNDAY, 11 MARCH 1750.[2] I should willingly have spent more time at Bristol, finding more and more proofs that God was reviving his work, but that the accounts I received from Ireland made me think it my duty to be there as soon as possible. So on MONDAY, 19 I set out with Christopher Hopper[3] for the New

[1] Publius Papinius Statius published his epic *Thebais* in 12 books *c*. A.D. 91. It took him twelve years to complete and tells the story of a quarrel between Eteocles and Polynices, the sons of Oedipus. *The Oxford Classical Dictionary*, 858.

[2] There is a discrepancy of a day in each entry between 19 and 25 Mar. in the original printed edition of the Journal.

[3] Hopper, one of Wesley's Preachers, refers to this journey in the brief account of his life which he wrote and which was published in the *Arm. Mag.* for 1781. Unfortunately, he had burnt the journal he had kept at the time, and relied very much on Wesley's account.

Passage. When we came there the wind was high and almost full against us. Nevertheless we crossed in less than two hours and reached Cardiff before night, where I preached at seven and found much refreshment.

TUESDAY, 20. Expecting to preach at Aberdare, sixteen Welsh miles from Cardiff, I rode thither over the mountains. But we found no notice had been given so, after resting an hour, we set out for Brecon. The rain did not intermit at all till we came within sight of it. Twice my horse fell down and threw me over his head, but without hurt either to man or beast.

WEDNESDAY, 21. We rode to Builth, where we found notice had been given that Howell Harris would preach at noon. By this means a large congregation was assembled, but Howell did not come so at their request I preached.[1] Between four and five Mr. Phillips[2] set out with us for Rhaeadr. I was much out of order in the morning; however, I held out to Llanidloes and then lay down. After an hour's sleep I was much better and rode on to Machynlleth.

About an hour and a half before we came to Dolgellau the heavy rain began. We were on the brow of the hill so we took all that came, our horses being able to go but half a foot pace. But we had amends made us at our inn. John Lewis and all his house gladly joined with us in prayer, and all we spoke to appeared willing to hear and to receive the truth in love.

FRIDAY, 23 Before we looked out we heard the roaring of the wind and the beating of the rain. We took horse at five. It rained incessantly all the way we rode. And when we came on the great mountain,[3] four miles from the town (by which time I was wet from my neck to my waist) it was with great difficulty I could avoid

---

[1] Hopper also 'spoke a few words' after Wesley; 'it was a time of love. The Welsh brethren rejoiced in the Lord' (*Arm. Mag.*, 1781, 91). Harris arrived 'near 2' and also preached. He then met the society and told them how God had 'brought Mr. Wesley here today to help bringing down Christ crucified'. Beynon, *Howell Harris, Reformer and Soldier*, 7.

[2] Edward Phillips, Maesmynys.

[3] Rhiniog Fawr and Rhiniog Fach.

being borne over my mare's head, the wind being ready to carry us all away. Nevertheless about ten we came safe to Tan-y-bwlch, praising Him who *saves both man and beast*. Our horses being well tired and ourselves thoroughly wet, we rested the remainder of the day, the rather because several of the family understood English, an uncommon thing in these parts. We spoke closely to them and they appeared much affected, particularly when we all joined in prayer.

SATURDAY, 24. We set out at five and at six came to the sands. But the tide was in so we could not pass. So I sat down in a little cottage for three or four hours and translated Aldrich's *Logic*.[1] About ten we passed and before five came to Moel y don ferry and found the boat ready for us. But the boatman desired us to stay a while, saying 'the wind was too high and the tide too strong'. The secret was they stayed for more passengers, and it was well they did, for while we were walking to and fro, Mr. Jenkin Morgan came, at whose house, near half-way between the ferry and Holyhead, I had lodged three years before. The night soon came on but our guide, knowing all the country, brought us safe to his own door.

SUNDAY, 25. I preached at Howell Thomas'[2] in Trefollwyn parish to a small earnest congregation. As many did not understand, one of the brethren repeated the substance of the sermon in Welsh. In the afternoon I went to William Prichard's,[3] though much

[1] Wesley's translation of Dr. Henry Aldrich's *Artis Logicae Compendium* (1691) was published later in the year, and was probably intended for the use of the pupils at Kingswood School. Tyerman, *Wesley*, ii. 90.

[2] Howell Thomas (b. 1698), the eldest of the three sons of Thomas Prichard (d. 1735) of Tŷ-gwyn near Llangefni. There is a strong tradition that, with his two brothers and sister, he occasionally made the long journey to Capel Helyg near Pwllheli to worship with the Independents there; the family may indeed have influenced William Prichard to leave Glasfryn Fawr farm for Penmynydd in Anglesey. Howell lived at Trefollwyn Goed (not parish) and evidently sympathized with Methodism, for apart from the welcome he gave Wesley, he had sustained an injury to his head in 1743 when trying to protect Benjamin Thomas, a Dissenter and a Methodist exhorter, from persecution at Minffordd. William Griffith, *Methodistiaeth Fore Môn*, 14 and in *J.H.S.P.C.W.* xxxviii. 33–4, 38.

[3] William Prichard (1702–73), of Penmynydd, Bodlew, and finally Clwchdernog, an Independent and a pioneer of Anglesey Nonconformity, *vide ante*, pp. xxv; 36 n. 1. John William Prichard (1749–1829), a gifted and versatile man of letters, was his son. *D.W.B.* s.n. William Prichard; *J.H.S.P.C.W.* xxxviii. 36–8.

against my will as there was none there to interpret and I was afraid very few of my hearers could understand English. But I was mistaken. The congregation was larger than I had ever seen in Anglesey, a considerable number of them understood English tolerably well, and the looks, sighs and gestures of those that did not showed that God was speaking to their hearts. It was a glorious opportunity. The whole congregation seemed to be melted down. So little do we know the extent of God's power! If He will work what shall hinder Him?

The wind being contrary I accepted of the invitation of an honest exciseman (Mr. Holloway) to stay at his house till it should change. Here I was in a little, quiet, solitary spot (*maxime animo exoptatum meo!*) where no human voice was heard but those of the family. On TUESDAY I desired Mr. Hopper to ride over to Holyhead and inquire concerning our passage. He brought word that we might possibly pass in a day or two, so on WEDNESDAY we both went thither. Here we overtook John Jane,[1] who had set out on foot from Bristol with three shillings in his pocket. Six nights out of the seven since he set out he had been entertained by utter strangers. He went by us, we could not tell how, and reached Holyhead on Sunday with one penny left.

By him we sent back our horses to Mr. Morgan's. I had a large congregation in the evening. It almost grieved me I could give them but one sermon now they were at length willing to hear. About eleven we were called to go on board, the wind being quite fair, and so it continued till we were just out of the harbour. It then turned west and blew a storm. There was neither moon nor stars but rain and wind enough, so that I was soon tired of staying on deck. But we met another storm below, for who should be there but the famous Mr. Gr.[2] of Caernarvonshire! A clumsy, overgrown, hard-faced man whose countenance I could only compare to that (which I saw in Drury Lane thirty years ago) of one of the ruffians in *Macbeth*.

[1] One of Wesley's Preachers. He died later that year after walking on an extremely hot day from Epworth to Hainton; 'all the money he had was one shilling and fourpence'. *Arm. Mag.*, 1779, 257.

[2] Hopper, too, omits, the Christian name but gives the surname in full as Griffith. No doubt he was William Griffith (d. 1752), the squire of Cefn Amwlch, Caernarvonshire, and the husband of the even more famous Madam Sidney Griffith, the friend of Howell Harris.

I was going to lie down when he tumbled in and poured out such a volley of ribaldry, obscenity and blasphemy, every second or third word being an oath, as was scarce ever heard at Billingsgate. Finding there was no room for me to speak, I retired into my cabin and left him to Mr. Hopper. Soon after, one or two of his own company interposed and carried him back to his cabin.

THURSDAY, 29. We wrought our way five or six leagues toward Ireland but were driven back in the afternoon to the very mouth of the harbour. Nevertheless the wind shifting one or two points, we ventured out again and by midnight we were got about half seas over. But the wind then turning full against us and blowing hard, we were driven back again and were glad about nine to get into the bay once more.

In the evening I was surprised to see, instead of some poor plain people, a room full of men daubed with gold and silver. That I might not go out of their depth I began expounding the story of Dives and Lazarus. It was more applicable than I was aware, several of them (as I afterwards learned) being eminently wicked men. I delivered my own soul, but they could in no wise bear it. One and another walked away murmuring sorely. Four stayed till I drew to a close. They then put on their hats and began talking to one another. I mildly reproved them, on which they rose up and went away, railing and blaspheming. I had then a comfortable hour with a company of plain honest Welshmen. In the night there was a violent storm. Blessed be God that we were safe on shore!

SATURDAY, 31. I determined to wait one week longer, and if we could not sail then to go and wait for a ship at Bristol. At seven in the evening, just as I was going down to preach, I heard a huge noise and took knowledge of the rabble of gentlemen. They had now strengthened themselves with drink and numbers and placed Captain Gr. (as they called him) at their head. He soon burst open both the outward and inner door, struck old Robert Griffith our landlord several times, kicked his wife, and with twenty full-mouthed oaths and curses demanded 'Where is the parson?'. Robert Griffith came up and desired me to go into another room, where he locked me in. The captain followed him quickly, broke open one or two doors, and got a chair to look on the top of a bed, but his foot slipping (as he was not a man made for climbing) he fell down backward all his length. He rose leisurely, turned about and, with his troop, walked away.

I then went down to a small company of the poor people and spent half an hour with them in prayer. About nine, as we were preparing to go to bed, the house was beset again. The captain burst in first. Robert Griffiths' daughter was standing in the passage with a pail full of water with which (whether with design or in her fright I know not) she covered him from head to foot. He cried as well as he could 'M . . .urder! Murder!' and stood very still for some moments. In the meantime, Robert Griffith stepped by him and locked the door. Finding himself alone, he began to change his voice and cry 'Let me out! let me out!'. Upon his giving his word and honour that none of the rest should come in, they opened the door and all went away together.

SUNDAY, 1 APRIL. We designed to set out early for Mr. Holloway's but the rain kept us till eight o'clock. We then set out, having one of Holyhead for our guide, reached a church[1] six or seven miles off about eleven (where we stopped till the service was ended) and went on to William Prichard's near Llannerch-y-medd.[2] I had appointed to preach there at four. I found the same spirit as before among this loving simple people. Many of our hearts burned within us, and I felt what I spoke, *The kingdom of God is at hand.*

Many who were come from the town earnestly pressed me to go and preach there, assuring me it was the general desire of the inhabitants. I felt a strong aversion to it but would not refuse, not knowing what God might have to do. So I went. But we were scarce set down when the *sons of Belial* from all parts gathered together and compassed the house. I could just understand their oaths and curses which were broad English and sounded on every side. The rest of their language was lost upon me, as mine was upon them. Our friends would have had me stayed within, but

---

[1] Possibly Llanynghenedl or Llanfachreth church.
[2] William Prichard had moved to Clwchdernog from Bodlew the previous year.

I judged it best to look them in the face while it was open day. So I bade them open the door, and Mr. Hopper and I walked straight through the midst of them. Having procured a guide, we then went on without hindrance to our retreat at Mr. Holloway's. Surely this journey will be for good, for hitherto we have had continual storm both by sea and land.

TUESDAY, 3. Mr. William Jones of Trefollwyn[1] called and told us an exhorter was preaching a little way off.[2] We went and found him on the common, standing on a little rock in the midst of an attentive congregation. After he had done, I preached and then returned to my study at Llangefni.

THURSDAY, 5. I read over a great part of Gerard's *Meditationes Sacrae*, a book recommended to me in the strongest terms. But alas! how was I disappointed. They have some masterly strokes but are in general trite and flat, the thoughts being as poor as the Latin. It is well every class of writers has a class of readers or they would never have come to a second impression.

About noon I preached two miles west of Llannerch-y-medd[3] and in the evening about a quarter of a mile further.[4] Not one scoffer is found in these congregations but whoever hears, hears for his life.

FRIDAY, 6. I preached near Llannerch-y-medd at noon and at Trefollwyn in the evening. Observing at night the wind was changed I rode to Holyhead early in the morning. A ship was just ready to sail, so we went on board and in the evening landed at Dublin.

[1] William Jones lived at Trefollwyn *Blas*, Howell Thomas at Trefollwyn *Goed*.

[2] Possibly John Powell or John Belcher; the former had been deputed by the Association to set out for North Wales at the beginning of March, the latter a month later. Griffith, *Methodistiaeth Fore Môn*, 109-10.

[3] Probably at Nantannog, the home of William Lloyd, who married the daughter of William Prichard, Clwchdernog. Griffith, op. cit. 69.

[4] Probably at Glan-y-gors.

XIX

27–31 AUGUST 1753

Bristol · New Passage · Cardiff · Fonmon · Cardiff · Bristol

MONDAY, 27. I came early to the New Passage [from Bristol], but the wind shifting obliged me to wait near six hours. When we were almost over it shifted again so that we could not land till between six and seven.

TUESDAY, 28. I reached Cardiff. Finding I had all here to begin anew I set out as at first by preaching in the Castle yard on *Lord, are there few that be saved?* I afterwards met what was once a society, and in the morning spoke severally to a few who were still desirous to join together and build up, not devour, one another.

I preached in the evening at Fonmon, and on THURSDAY, 30 spake to many at Cardiff who were resolved to set out once more in the Bible way and strengthen each other's hands in God.

FRIDAY, 31. We had a pleasant ride and a ready passage so that we reached Bristol in the afternoon.

XX

18–29 MARCH 1756

Coleford · Brecon · Trefeca · Brecon · Builth · Rhaeadr
Dolgellau · Tan-y-bwlch · Caernarfon · Moel y don
Holyhead · Howth

THURSDAY, 18 MARCH 1756. We rode [from Coleford] through hard rain to Brecon, and came just at the hour appointed for preaching. The Town Hall, in which I was desired to preach, is a large and commodious place,[1] and the whole congregation

---

[1] It still stands in the High Street, and, apart from the removal of the iron railings in the archways and two doorways, and the substitution of windows in 1888, it still

(one poor gentleman excepted) behaved with seriousness and decency.

FRIDAY, 19. I rode over to Howell Harris at Trefeca,[1] though not knowing how to get any farther. But he helped us out of our difficulties, offering to send one with us who would show us the way and bring our horses back. So I then determined to go on to Holyhead, after spending a day or two at Brecon.

SATURDAY, 20. It being the day appointed for the Justices and Commissioners to meet, the town was extremely full. And curiosity (if no better motive) brought most of the gentlemen to the preaching. Such another opportunity could not have been of speaking to all the rich and great of the county. And they all appeared to be serious and attentive. Perhaps one or two may lay it to heart.

SUNDAY, 21. I delayed preaching till nine for the sake of the tender and delicate ones. At two we had near the whole town, and God reserved the great blessing for the last. Afterwards we rode to Trefeca. But our guide was ill so in the morning we set out without him.

Before I talked with him myself I wondered H. Harris did not go out and preach as usual. But he now informed me he preached till he could preach no longer, his constitution being entirely broken. While he was thus confined he was pressed in spirit to build a large house, though he knew not why or for whom. But as soon as it was built men, women and children without his seeking came to it from all parts of Wales. And except in the case of the Orphan House at Halle, I never heard of so many signal interpositions of Divine Providence.

MONDAY, 22. It continued fair till we came to Builth, where I preached to the usual congregation. Mr. Phillips[2] then guided us

retains its outward appearance of Wesley's day. Internally, however, the basement beneath the old Assembly Room (in which Wesley probably preached) and Council Room has been completely transformed. Apparently the building was also used as a Shire Hall until the new Shire Hall was built in Glamorgan Street in 1842. T. Jones, *Hist. of Brecknock*, i. 132, 135, 144, 149, 166.

[1] This was Wesley's first meeting with Harris since the Disruption of 1750.
[2] Edward Phillips, Maesmynys.

to Rhaeadr, about fourteen English miles. It snowed hard behind us on both sides, but not at all where we were.

TUESDAY, 23. When we took horse there was nothing to be seen but a waste of white, the snow covering both hills and vales. As we could see no path, it was not without much difficulty as well as danger that we went on. But between seven and eight the sun broke out and the snow began to melt. So we thought all our difficulty was over till, about nine, the snow fell faster than ever. In an hour it changed into hail which, as we rode over the mountains, drove violently in our face. About twelve this turned into hard rain followed by an impetuous wind. However, we pushed on through all, and before sunset came to Dolgellau.

Here we found everything we wanted except sleep, of which we were deprived by a company of drunken, roaring sea-captains who kept possession of the room beneath us till between two and three in the morning, so that we did not take horse till after six. And then we could make no great speed, the frost being exceeding sharp and much ice on the road. Hence we were not able to reach Tan-y-bwlch till between eleven and twelve. An honest Welshman here gave us to know (though he spoke no English) that he was just going over the sands, so we hastened on with him and by that means came in good time to Caernarfon.

Here we passed a quiet and comfortable night and took horse about six in the morning. Supposing, after we had rode near an hour, that a little house on the other side was the ferry-house, we went down to the water and called amain, but we could not procure any answer. In the meantime it began to rain hard, though the wind was extremely high. Finding none would come over, we went to a little church[1] which stood near for shelter. We had waited about an hour when a woman and a girl came into the churchyard, whom I did not mind, supposing they could speak no English. They were following a sheep which ran close to us. I then asked, 'Is not this Moel y don ferry?'. The girl answered, 'Moel y don ferry! No, the ferry is two miles further'. So we might have called long enough. When we came to Moel y don the wind fell, the sky cleared up,

---

[1] Llanfair-is-gaer church.

the boat came over without delay, and soon landed us in Anglesey. On our way to Holyhead one met and informed us that the packet sailed the night before. I said, 'Perhaps it may carry me for all that'. So we pushed on and came thither in the afternoon. The packet did sail the night before and got more than half-seas over, but the wind turning against them and blowing hard, they were glad to get back this afternoon. I scarce ever remember so violent a storm as blew all the night long. The wind continued contrary the next day.

SUNDAY, 28. About nine in the morning I spent some time with a few serious people, and gave notice of preaching at four in the afternoon, as soon as the evening service was ended. It began soon after three. Ten minutes before four Mr. E.[1] began catechizing the children in Welsh. I stayed till after five. As there was no sign of his concluding I then went home and found the people waiting, to whom I expounded those solemn words, *Watch and pray always, that ye may be counted worthy to escape all these things which are coming upon the earth.*

MONDAY, 29. We left the harbour about twelve, having six or seven officers and abundance of passengers on board. The wind was full west and there was great possibility of a stormy night. So it was judged best to put back. But one gentleman making a motion to try a little longer, in a short time brought all over to his opinion. So they agreed to go out and 'look for a wind'. The wind continued westerly all the night. Nevertheless in the morning we were within two leagues of Ireland! Between nine and ten I landed at Howth and walked on for Dublin.[2]

[1] The Revd. Thomas Ellis, vicar of Holyhead. Curnock (iv. 154) has 'Mr. D.'— a misprint for the 'Mr. E.' of the first edition of the Journal.

[2] While he was delayed at Holyhead, John Wesley wrote to Howell Harris and gave him a dissertation on the dangers of self-will. 'O Howell, Let us be more & more aware of this deadly enemy. It contains Passion, Stubborness, Unpersuadableness, & what not? O let us give it no Quarter! The Lord make us mild, quiet, loving, patient of Reproof, Advice, Contradiction, Contempt: Willing to suffer all things for his name's sake!'. After delivering himself thus and signing himself 'Your very Affectionate Brother', he added a postscript with which all later students of Harris's handwriting will heartily concur: 'When you write, have Patience. For sometimes you write so hastily that I can't read it.' *W.H.S. Proc.* xxiv. 89.

XXI

12–14 AUGUST 1756

Dublin · Holyhead · Bangor · Penmaen-mawr · Conway
Llansanffraid Glan Conwy · Holywell · Chester

SUNDAY, 8 AUGUST 1756. We were to sail [from Dublin], the wind being fair, but as we were going aboard it turned full east. I find it of great use to be in suspense; it is an excellent means of breaking our will. May we be ready either to stay longer on this shore or to launch into eternity.

On TUESDAY evening I preached my farewell sermon. Mr. Walsh[1] did the same in the morning. We then walked to the quay, but it was still a doubt whether we were to sail or no, Sir T. P. having sent word to the captain of the packet that if the wind was fair he would go over, and it being his custom (*hominis magnificentiam!*) to keep the whole ship to himself. But the wind coming to the east, he would not go, so about noon we went on board. In two or three hours we reached the mouth of the harbour. It then fell calm. We had five cabin passengers beside Mr. [Thomas] Walsh, [John] Haughton,[2] [James] Morgan[3] and me. They were all civil and tolerably serious. The sailors likewise behaved uncommonly well.

THURSDAY, 12. About eight we began singing on the quarter deck, which soon drew all our fellow-passengers as well as the captain with the greatest part of his men. I afterwards gave an

---

[1] It may have been on this journey that Thomas Walsh (the best Hebrew scholar Wesley had ever known), 'finding that in many places they [the natives of Wales] did not understand English . . . felt great concern on that occasion and formed a resolution, if his life and health permitted, he would learn the Welsh language for their sakes'. Jackson (ed.), *E.M.P.* iii. 119. Walsh was an Irishman who could preach in Erse. Unfortunately, his 'life and health' did not permit him to carry out his resolution, for he died in 1758.

[2] John Haughton attended the Bristol Association in Jan. 1747 (*ante*, p. xxviii). At Cork on one occasion, when the mob were burning an effigy of Wesley, he threw up the window and began to preach to them. He later took Holy Orders and settled in Ireland. Tyerman, *Wesley*, i. 459.

[3] A well-read and popular Preacher to whom Wesley bequeathed his watch in 1768 n one of the several wills he made. Tyerman, *Wesley*, iii. 16, 23, 41.

exhortation. We then spent some time in prayer. They all kneeled down with us. Nor did their seriousness wear off all the day. About nine we landed at Holyhead after a pleasant passage of twenty-three hours.

FRIDAY, 13. Having hired horses for Chester, we set out about seven. Before one we reached Bangor, the situation of which is delightful beyond expression. Here we saw a large and handsome cathedral, but no trace of the good old monks of Bangor, so many hundreds of whom fell a sacrifice at once to cruelty and revenge.[1] The country from hence to Penmaen-mawr is far pleasanter than any garden. Mountains of every shape and size, vales clothed with grass or corn, woods and smaller tufts of trees were continually varying on the one hand, as was the sea prospect on the other. Penmaen-mawr itself rises almost perpendicular to an enormous height from the sea. The road runs along the side of it, so far above the beach that one could not venture to look down but that there is a wall built all along, about four feet high. Meantime, the ragged cliff hangs over one's head as if it would fall every moment.[2] An hour after we had left this awful place we came to the ancient town of Conway.[3] It is walled round and the walls are in tolerably good repair. The castle is the noblest ruin I ever saw. It is four square and has four large round towers on each side, the inside of which have been stately apartments. One side of the castle is a large church, the windows and arches of which have been curiously wrought.[4]

[1] Wesley was here confusing Bangor (Caernarvonshire) with Bangor Is-coed (or Bangor-on-Dee, Flintshire). The reference is to the monks from the monastery at Bangor Is-coed who were massacred by Ethelfrith of Northumbria at the battle of Chester in A.D. 613.

[2] Many travellers in North Wales (including the redoubtable Dr. Samuel Johnson) were overawed by and somewhat nervous of 'this awful place' before the new road over Penmaen-mawr was constructed in 1772 with financial assistance from private citizens in Dublin and even from the Irish Parliament. A. H. Dodd in *Arch. Camb.*, 1925, 130.

[3] To reach Llansanffraid Glan Conwy from Penmaen-mawr, Wesley was obliged to cross the river Conway by ferry at Conway or at Tal-y-cafn, for Telford's bridge was not constructed until 1823.

[4] Though Wesley's appraisal of Edward I's castle at Conway was thoroughly sound (for it is still one of the finest examples of military architecture in Europe), he probably mistook the Great Hall for the church (or chapel). The chapel was placed in what is still known as the Chapel Tower.

An arm of the sea runs round two sides of the hill on which the castle stands—once the delight of kings, now overgrown with thorns and inhabited by doleful birds only.

About eight we reached Plas Bach where, as soon as I named my name, William Roberts received us with all gladness.[1] But neither he nor any of his family could speak one sentence of English. Yet our guide helped us out pretty well. After supper we sang and went to prayers. Though they could not speak it, most of them understood English, and God spoke to their hearts.

SATURDAY, 14. Several of the neighbours came early in the morning and gladly received a few words of exhortation. We then rode on through one of the pleasantest countries in the world, by Holywell to Chester. Here we had a comfortable meeting in the evening, as well as the next day, both in the room[3] and in the Square.

XXII

9-11 AUGUST 1758

Queenstown · Pen-clawdd · Swansea · Pyle · Cardiff · Bristol

TUESDAY, 8 AUGUST 1758. I preached not far from the beach [at Queenstown] to a very decent and serious congregation. Presently after, a vessel sailed by, bound for Wales. We went on board without delay, got out of the harbour by eleven, and by

---

[1] William Roberts of Plas Bach, Llansanffraid Glan Conwy, was a Calvinistic Methodist. Converted by Peter Williams in 1748, he supported Howell Harris in the Disruption of 1750, and in 1759 he moved with his wife and younger children to Y Geuffordd near Talgarth in Breconshire. His son Thomas joined his mother on his father's death, 25 May 1760, and in 1762 moved to Chancefield and thence, in 1773, to Trefeca to join Howell Harris's Family and to become later one of its trustees. *D.W.B.*, s.n. Thomas Roberts; *J.H.S.P.C.W.* xli. 14–19; xliv. 38–40; xlviii. 4–11. Probably Wesley had been told of William Roberts by Howell Harris at Trefeca the previous March. *W.H.S. Proc.* xxiv. 89. One of Roberts's granddaughters married Edward Linnell, an exciseman from Llansannan, who later entered the Wesleyan Methodist ministry. John Hughes in *W.M. Mag.*, 1832, 472–3 (where John Roberts the son is confused with William the father).

[2] The 'room' at Chester was a barn, first rented early in 1752 and re-erected later in the year after it had been destroyed by the mob. F. F. Bretherton, *Early Methodism in and around Chester*, 29–35.

WEDNESDAY noon were abreast of the Isle of Lundy. But we had not yet done our work, for the wind fell and we did not get into the river till near sunset. Observing three or four sailors then standing together, I began explaining to them the nature of religion. In a few minutes all within the ship came together, and without the ceremony of naming a text I enlarged on *The kingdom of heaven is not meat and drink but righteousness and peace and joy in the Holy Ghost*. About eleven we landed at Pen-clawdd, and in the morning rode to Swansea.

THURSDAY, 10. We rode through a pleasant country to Pyle. We were setting out from thence when a violent shower drove us into the house[1] again and constrained us to talk with two or three travellers. I believe our labour was not lost, for they appeared to be greatly affected. I preached at Cardiff in the evening and the next morning. We reached the Passage about noon. But they did not tell us till half-hour after five that the boat would not pass that night. With much difficulty I procured a small boat to carry us over, leaving our horses behind. Landing soon after six, we walked on and between nine and ten came to Bristol.

XXIII

21 AUGUST–2 SEPTEMBER 1758

Bristol · Cardiff · Fonmon · Cowbridge · Llan-maes · Fonmon
Pyle · Neath · Swansea · Newton · Swansea · Neath
Margam · Cowbridge · Cardiff · Bristol

THURSDAY, 17 AUGUST 1758. I went to the cathedral [at Bristol] to hear Mr. Handel's *Messiah*.[2] I doubt if that congregation

---

[1] Possibly the Old [Wine] House Inn (which is still standing—opposite St. James's church, on the A. 48 from Bridgend to Port Talbot).

[2] First successfully performed in Dublin in 1742, Handel's *Messiah* was withdrawn after its third performance in England. Its popularity dates from its revival at the Foundling Hospital in 1749. A. S. Turberville (ed.), *Johnson's England*, ii. 195.

was ever so serious at a sermon as they were during this performance. In many parts, especially several of the choruses, it exceeded my expectation.

Having promised to take a little journey into Wales, on MONDAY the 21st I set out with Joseph Jones.[1] We were in the boat before nine, but did not land our horses till a quarter before three. However I reached Cardiff [in] time enough to preach in the room, though not in the Castle.

TUESDAY, 22. I gathered up as well as I could the fragments of the society. At six in the evening I preached in the Castle.

WEDNESDAY, 23. We rode to Fonmon. The behaviour of Mr. Jones surprised me.[2] It seemed as if he inherited the spirit of his father. I preached at seven to a deeply serious congregation, and to a good part of them at five in the morning.

THURSDAY, 24. I wrote a second letter to Dr. Free, the warmest opponent I have had for many years. I leave him now to laugh and scold and witticise and call names just as he pleases, for I have done.[3]

FRIDAY, 25. I rode to Cowbridge, and preached at three in the afternoon in the new Assembly Room.[4] I observed no trifler there, though there were several of the better rank. About six, I preached in a green court at Llan-maes to a company of right old simple

---

[1] One of Wesley's Preachers, who ceased itinerating in 1760. Tyerman, *Wesley*, i. 460.

[2] Robert Jones (the third), the only surviving son of the Methodist squire. Wesley's opinion of him was rather premature (as he realized later—*post*, pp. 67; 117 n. 1). As a boy he ran away (understandably!) from Kingswood School in 1749, and in later years his extravagant mode of living obliged him to seek refuge in France from his creditors. *Wesley Letters*: 8–13; 16; 22; A. G. Ives, *Kingswood School*, 35–9.

[3] The Revd. Dr. Free was vicar of East Coker in Somerset, Thursday lecturer at St. Mary Hill, London, and lecturer at Newington, Surrey, 'an everlasting pamphleteer of the most scurrilous genus' (Tyerman, *Wesley*, ii. 321). Wesley may have shown his 'second letter' to John Hodges, for on 4 Sept. Hodges gave him his opinion of it in a letter which does him much credit, and which Wesley published in the *Arminian Magazine*, 1780, 106–7 (reprinted in *Bathafarn*, xxiii. 25).

[4] The upper room of the former E. John's Corn Stores in the High Street, near the Bear Hotel.

Christians.[1] I could not get from them so soon as I designed, so that we did not reach Fonmon till near nine.

SATURDAY, 26. One undertook to guide me the nearest way into the main road, but in five or six miles he lost his way, so that for some time we wandered upon the mountains.[2] About noon, however, we got into the road, and an hour and a half after to Pyle. Before we left it I spoke a few words to the woman of the house.[3] She seemed quite struck. How few words suffice when God applies them to the heart!

I knew not where to go at Neath,[4] but as we entered the town a man fixed his eyes upon me (though he had never seen me before) and said, 'Sir, that is the house where the preachers put up their horses'. I had been there only a few minutes when another came in and said, 'Sir, Mrs. Morgan expects you. I will show you the way'. To Mrs. Morgan's we went and were as cordially received as if she had known us twenty years. It was market-day, so I preached about five in the room, a large commodious place. I believe most that were present (several of whom were backsliders) felt that God was there.

SUNDAY, 27. We reached Swansea at seven and were met by one who conducted us to his house and thence to a kind of castle in which was a green court surrounded by high old walls.[5] A large congregation assembled soon and behaved with the utmost decency. A very uncommon blessing was among them, as uses to be among them that are simple of heart. The congregation was considerably more than doubled at five in the afternoon. Many gay and

---

[1] Philip Thomas's society at Llan-maes had by now thrown in its lot with Wesley, for it appears in the *Min. of Conf.* in 1748. The green court may have belonged to the house known later as Tile House, which then belonged to the Plaisted family, who were Wesleyan Methodists and who later gave the lower part of the Brown Lion (now Maliphant House) for the use of the society. Jane Thomas, a member of the society, left John Wesley a legacy and appointed him one of the trustees of her Will. *Centenary Brochure of the Wesleyan Methodist Church, Llantwit Major*, 6; *Bathafarn*, xii. 51–3.

[2] A slip of the pen or memory, for there are no mountains between Fonmon and Pyle.

[3] Probably the inn at which he had stayed on 10 Aug. 1758.

[4] Wesley had not been to Neath since 18–19 Aug. 1746.

[5] Probably Swansea castle rather than Oystermouth castle, overlooking Swansea Bay.

well-dressed persons were among them, but they were as serious as the poorest. Peter Jaco,[1] who was driven to us by contrary winds, was agreeably surprised at them.

MONDAY, 28. I scarce ever saw such rain in Europe as we had for a considerable part of this morning. In one of the main streets the water ran with a stream capable of turning a mill. However, having appointed to preach at Newton,[2] about six miles from Swansea, I was determined not to break my word though I supposed but few would attend. But I was mistaken; such a number of people came together as no house in the town could contain. A barn was soon prepared, and it pleased God to send a gracious rain upon their hearts.

After preaching in Swansea in the evening, I met those who desired to join in society and explained to them the nature and design of it, with which they were quite unacquainted.[3]

TUESDAY, 29. I rode back to Neath in order to put the society there (an unlicked mass) into some form. This on Saturday they had begged me to do, but they seemed now to have quite forgotten it. Mr. Evans, the Presbyterian minister, had turned them upside down.[4] They looked as if they had never seen me before, all but five or six, who were much ashamed of their brethren.

WEDNESDAY, 30. I rode on to Margam. There used to be preaching here till Lord Mansel, dying without children, left the estate to Mr. Talbot. He forbade all his tenants to receive the preachers and so effectively put a stop to it. But he did not glory in it long. A few months after, God called him home.[5]

---

[1] One of Wesley's Preachers, then on his way to Ireland.

[2] Now a suburb of Swansea, about a mile west of Mumbles.

[3] Rarely can one point to the date of formation of a Wesleyan Methodist society in Wales, but that at Swansea was evidently formed on 28 Aug. 1758.

[4] *Possibly* William Evans, minister of Cwm-mawr and Rhydymaerdy in the parish of Llanrhidian from 1754 to 1770 and of his native Cwmllynfell as well from 1767. A moderate Calvinist and an evangelical preacher who added over 150 members to the church at Cwmllynfell in less than three years; died 1770, aged 54. *D.W.B.*, s.n.; J. Dyfnallt Owen, J. B. Jones, and Ben Davies, *Hanes Eglwys Cwmllynfell*, 17.

[5] Wesley seems to have been a little confused here. It was Christopher, the 3rd Baron Mansel, who died within a few months of succeeding to the title in 1744; his

At noon I preached again in the Assembly room at Cowbridge; in the castle at Cardiff in the evening.

THURSDAY, 31. I talked with several of the people and found the old spirit reviving. In the evening I preached in the Town Hall. Several eminent sinners were present, and God was present in an uncommon manner, as also at the meeting of the society.

FRIDAY, 1 SEPTEMBER. After a busy and comfortable day, I preached once more in the Castle. The word seemed to sink deep into the hearers, though many of them were of the genteeler sort. In the society we were much refreshed. Many followed me to Thomas Glascott's house, where two or three were cut to the heart, particularly both his daughters, and cried to God with strong cries and tears.

SATURDAY, 2. We rode to the New Passage, crossed over in half an hour, and about five came to Bristol.

XXIV

2 MAY 1759

Chester · Mold · Chester

WEDNESDAY, 2 MAY 1759. I rode over [from Chester] to Mold in Flintshire, about twelve miles from Chester. The sun was very hot and the wind very cold, but as the place they had chosen for me was exposed both to the sun and the wind, the one balanced the other. And notwithstanding the Chester races (which had drawn the rich away) and the market-day (which detained many of the

---

nephew, the Revd. Thomas Talbot, the absentee rector of Collingbourne in Wiltshire, who succeeded Bussy Mansel, the 4th Baron, in 1750, lived until 1758—he was buried at Margam on 9 Mar. only a few months prior to Wesley's visit. A. Leslie Evans, *Margam Abbey*, 114, 134–5; Williams, *Sheriffs of Glamorgan*, 64–6; Patricia Moore in *Glamorgan Historian* (ed. Stewart Williams), iv. 23–4. (Curnock, iv. 284 n. 2 is very wide of the mark.)

poor), we had a multitude of people, the serious part of whom soon influenced the rest, so that all but two or three remained uncovered and kneeled down as soon as I began to pray.[1]

THURSDAY, 3. We crossed over from Chester to Liverpool.

XXV

25 MARCH 1760

Chester · Mold · Little Leigh

TUESDAY, 25 MARCH 1760. I rode to Mold in Flintshire. The wind was often ready to bear away both man and horse, but the earnest, serious congregation rewarded us for our trouble.

WEDNESDAY, 26. About nine I preached at Little Leigh, a mile or two from Northwich.

XXVI

3 APRIL 1761

Chester · Mold · Chester

FRIDAY, 3 APRIL 1761. I preached about one at Mold in Flintshire and was again obliged to preach abroad,[2] though the wind was exceeding rough. All were deeply attentive. I preached in the evening at Chester, and in the morning set out for Liverpool.

[1] The fact that preparations had been made for Wesley's visit may point to the existence of a society at Mold at this time. If so, it may have been formed by Thomas Olivers, a native of Tregynon and one of Wesley's Preachers, who was stationed at Chester in 1758–9. There was certainly a society there in 1762, and as Wesley paid three specific visits to the town in successive years it is more than likely that it existed in 1759. *Welsh Wes. Meth.* 46.

[2] The previous day Wesley had had to preach in the open-air at Tattenhall because the house was too small to contain the congregation.

XXVII

29 MARCH 1762

Bristol · Chepstow · Hereford

MONDAY, 29 MARCH 1762. I came to the New Passage a little before nine. The rain and wind increased much while we were on the water; however, we were safe on shore at ten. I preached, about twelve, in the New Room at Chepstow.[1] One of the congregation was a neighbouring clergyman, who lived in the same staircase with me at Christ Church, and was then far more serious than me. Blessed be God, who has looked upon me at last! *Now* let me redeem the time!

In the afternoon, we had such a storm of hail as I scarce ever saw in my life. The roads likewise were so extremely bad that we did not reach Hereford till past eight.[2]

XXVIII

17–31 AUGUST 1763

Bristol · New Passage · Chepstow · Coleford · Monmouth
Crickhowell · Brecon · Trefeca · Brecon · Trecastle
Carmarthen · St. Clears · Laugharne · Tenby · Pembroke
Haverfordwest · St. Clears · Llanelli · Loughor ferry · Swansea
Cowbridge · Llandaf · Wenvoe · Cardiff · Llandaf · Aberthaw
Fonmon · Cardiff · Chepstow · Old Passage · Bristol

WEDNESDAY, 17 AUGUST 1763. Being informed that the boat at the Old Passage would go over at six o'clock, I took horse at four and came to the Passage a few minutes after six. But they told us they would not pass till twelve, and I had appointed to

---

[1] On 31 May 1761 Howell Harris (then in the militia) preached to the soldiers at Chepstow 'and to some that begin to meet in this town together'—which may point to the origins of the Chepstow society. Beynon, *Howell Harris, Reformer and Soldier*, 117.

[2] Turnpike Trusts were not formed in Monmouthshire until 1755. J. Conway Davies in *Presenting Monmouthshire*, ii, No. 4, 31–8.

preach in Chepstow at eleven. So we thought it best to try the New Passage. We came thither at seven and might possibly have stayed till noon had not an herd of oxen come just in time to the other side. In the boat which brought them over we crossed the water, and got to Chepstow between ten and eleven. As it had rained almost all the day, the house contained the congregation. Hence we rode to Coleford. The wind being high, I consented to preach in their new room; but large as it was, it would not contain the people, who appeared to be not a little affected, of which they gave a sufficient proof by filling the room at five in the morning.

THURSDAY, 18. We breakfasted at a friend's a mile or two from Monmouth and rode to Crickhowell, where I intended to dine; but I found other work to do. Notice had been given that I would preach, and some were come many miles to hear. So I began without delay, and I did not observe one light or inattentive person in the congregation. When we came to Brecon we found it was the Assize week, so that I could not have the Town Hall as before, the court being to sit there at the very time when I had appointed to preach. So I preached at Mr. James' door, and all the people behaved as in the presence of God.[1]

FRIDAY, 19. I preached near the market-place, and afterwards rode over to Trefeca. Howell Harris' house is one of the most elegant places which I have ever seen in Wales.[2] The little chapel and all things round about it are finished in an uncommon taste, and the gardens, orchards, fish-ponds and mount adjoining make

---

[1] Probably Thomas James, the Brecon attorney. The Brecon society may have met at first in his house. T. Wynne Jones, *Wesleyan Methodism in the Brecon Circuit*, 84; *J.H.S.P.C.W.* lv. 65.

[2] Harris, who had invited Wesley to Trefeca the previous 25 July, had made considerable improvements to Trefeca since his last visit in Mar. 1756. He went to meet Wesley at Brecon on 18 Aug., and on the following day he wrote in his Diary: 'Att 10, Mr. Jn. Wesley graced our Chappel with an Excellent Exposition on ye History of David killing Goliath. We were happy att Dinner . . . I went with him to Brecon with my Wife and Hannah [Bowen] and Betty [his daughter] to shew Love to him openly. He preached in ye Street [Struet] an excellent Sermon. I had freedom to press on him to stand firm in ye Established Church.' *J.H.S.P.C.W.* xxxiii. 21; Beynon, op. cit. 186, 192. Thomas Tobias, one of Wesley's Preachers, arrived at Trefeca and preached on the evening of 18 Aug.

the place a little paradise. He thanks God for these things and looks through them. About six-score persons are now in the Family—all diligent, all constantly employed, all fearing God and working righteousness. I preached at ten to a crowded audience, and in the evening at Brecon again, but to the poor only, the rich (a very few excepted) were otherwise employed.

SATURDAY, 20. We took horse at four, and rode through one of the pleasantest countries in the world. When we came to Trecastle, we had rode fifty miles in Monmouthshire and Breconshire; and I will be bold to say all England does not afford such a line of fifty miles' length for fields, meadows, brooks and gently rising mountains, fruitful to the very top. Carmarthenshire, into which we came soon after, has at least as fruitful a soil, but it is not so pleasant because it has fewer mountains, though abundance of brooks and rivers. About five I preached on the Green[1] at Carmarthen to a large number of deeply attentive people. Here two gentlemen[2] from Pembroke met me, with whom we rode to St. Clears, intending to lodge there. But the inn was quite full so we concluded to try for Laugharne, though we knew not the way and it was now quite dark. Just then came up an honest man who was riding thither and we willingly bore him company.

SUNDAY, 21. It rained almost all the morning. However, we reached Tenby about eleven. The rain then ceased and I preached at the cross to a congregation gathered from many miles round. The sun broke out several times and shone hot in my face, but never for two minutes together. About five I preached to a far larger

---

[1] The Green, according to M. H. Jones, was 'an open strip of land at the end of the castle courtyard, facing the bridge over the river Tywi, and enclosed within living memory'. *W.H.S. Proc.* ix. 89.

[2] One of them may have been John Barnes, paymaster of the fort at Pembroke and a former Moravian, for according to Nyberg, the Moravian Labourer at Haverfordwest, it was he 'who first introduced Mr. Wesley's party into Pembrokeshire'. *W.H.S. Proc.* xii. 46–7. In 1765 Barnes (of Carmarthen by then) published 'The Christian's Pocket Companion: consisting of select Texts of the New Testament, with suitable observations in prose and verse'. The Preface to it was written by John Wesley from 'Pembroke, July 30, 1764', and according to David Young, the book was published in Welsh the following year (*Origin*, 245). Tyerman, *Wesley*, ii. 552; Richard Green, *Wesley Bibliography*, no. 231.

congregation at Pembroke. A few gay people behaved ill at the beginning, but in a short time they lost their gaiety and were as serious as their neighbours.

WEDNESDAY, 24. I rode over to Haverfordwest.[1] Finding it was the Assize week, I was afraid the bulk of the people would be too busy to think about hearing sermons. But I was mistaken. I have not seen so numerous a congregation since I set out of London, and they were one and all deeply attentive. Surely some will bring forth fruit.

THURSDAY, 25. I was more convinced than ever that the preaching like an apostle, without joining together those that are awakened and training them up in the ways of God, is only begetting children for the murderer. How much preaching has there been for these twenty years all over Pembrokeshire![2] But no regular societies, no discipline, no order or connexion, and the consequence is that nine in ten of the once-awakened are now faster asleep than ever.

FRIDAY, 26. We designed to take horse at four, but the rain poured down so that one could scarce look out. About six, however, we set out and rode through heavy rain to St. Clears. Having then little hopes of crossing the sands, we determined to go round by Carmarthen, but the hostler told us we might save several miles by going to Llanstephan ferry. We came thither about noon, where a good woman informed us that the boat was aground and would not pass till the evening; so we judged it best to go by Carmarthen still. But when we had rode three or four miles, I recollected that I had heard speak of a ford which would save us some miles' riding. We inquired of an old man, who soon mounted his horse, showed us the way, and rode through the river before us.

[1] 'Aug. 23, 1763. Br. Nyberg at his return to Haverfordwest heard that Mr. John Wesley has yesterday notified by the Town-Crier that he would preach in this Town next Wednesday (at the very hour of our preaching) tho' he has not one acquaintance here.' G. M. Roberts, 'Gleanings from the Moravian Records, Haverfordwest', in *J.H.S.P.C.W.* xxxvii. 44.
[2] South Pembrokeshire had certainly witnessed much evangelical activity during the previous twenty years by the Welsh Calvinistic Methodists and the Moravians, but no evidence has come to light to suggest that Wesley's Preachers had been active there for so long.

Soon after, my mare dropped a shoe, which occasioned so much loss of time that we could not ride the sands but were obliged to go round, through a miserable road, to Llanelli.[1] To mend the matter, our guide lost his way, both before we came to Llanelli and after, so that it was as much as we could do to reach Loughor ferry a little after sunset. Knowing it was impossible then to preach at Penrice[3] as we designed, we went on straight to Swansea.

SATURDAY, 27. I preached at seven to one or two hundred people, many of whom seemed full of good desires, but as there is no society, I expect no deep or lasting work.

Mr. Evans[3] now gave us an account from his own knowledge of what has made a great noise in Wales. 'It is common in the congregations attended by Mr. W. W.[4] and one or two other clergymen, after preaching is over, for anyone who has a mind to give out a verse of a hymn. This they sing over and over with all their might, perhaps above thirty, yea forty times. Meanwhile, the bodies of two or three, sometimes ten or twelve, are violently agitated, and they leap up and down in all manner of postures, frequently for hours together.' I think there needs no great penetration to understand this. They are honest, upright men who really feel the love of God in their hearts, but they have little experience either of the ways of God or the devices of Satan. So he serves himself of their simplicity in order to wear them out and bring discredit on the work of God.[5]

[1] The first edition of the Journal has 'Lanellos' which Curnock interpreted as 'Llandyfaelog', though he preferred 'Llanelli' for the same name in the next sentence. There was at that time no bridge over the river Loughor.

[2] The first edition of the Journal reads 'to reach at Penrice', which makes no sense; Curnock assumed Wesley to mean 'to reach Penrice'. But as Wesley could conceivably have *reached* Penrice that evening, but not early enough to preach there, 'reach' is possibly a misprint for 'preach'.

[3] Doubtless the person whom he had met in 1758. Whoever he was, he could not have been John Evans, author of *A Sketch of the Denominations of the Christian World* (as Curnock suggested, op. cit., v. 27 n. 2) for he was not born until 1767. Curnock evidently misread Tyerman, who was quoting, not from *A Sketch*, but from Lloyd's *Evening Post* for 27 June 1763, which referred to the 'Jumpers' of Llan-crwys. Tyerman, *Wesley*, ii. 480–1.

[4] Revd. William Williams, Pantycelyn, whose collection of hymns, *Caniadau y rhai sydd ar y Môr o Wydr*, is said to have occasioned the revival which first broke out at Llangeitho in 1762 and then spread to many other parts of Wales. R. Geraint Gruffydd in *J.H.S.P.C.W.* liv. 68–75; lv. 4–13.

[5] Wesley had witnessed similar physical manifestations as a result of his own preaching at Bristol as early as 1739.

About two I preached at Cowbridge in the Assembly Room, and then went on to Llandaf.[1] The congregation was waiting, so I began without delay, explaining to them *the righteousness of faith*. A man has need to be all fire who comes into these parts, where almost everyone is cold as ice. Yet God is able to warm their hearts and make rivers run in dry places.

SUNDAY, 28. I preached once more in Wenvoe church, but it was hard work. Mr. H.[2] read the prayers (not as he did once, with such fervour and solemnity as struck almost every hearer but) like one reading an old song, in a cold, dry, careless manner; and there was no singing at all. Oh what life was here once! But now there is not one spark left.

Thence I rode to Cardiff and found the society in as ruinous a condition as the castle. The same poison of mysticism has well-nigh extinguished the last spark of life here also. I preached in the Town Hall on *Now God commandeth all men everywhere to repent*. There was a little shaking among the dry bones; possibly some of them may yet *come together and live*.

MONDAY, 29. At noon I preached again at Llandaf, and in the evening at Aberthaw.[3] I found the most life in this congregation that I have found anywhere in Glamorgan. We lodged at F[onmon] Castle, so agreeable once, but how is the scene changed! How dull and unlovely is every place where there is nothing of God!

TUESDAY, 30. I preached in the castle at Cardiff and endeavoured to lift up the hands that hung down. A few seemed to awake and shake themselves from the dust. Let these go on and more will follow.

[1] Probably to Llandaf Court (now the Cathedral School), the home of the Mathews family. Thomas Mathews had married Diana, daughter of Robert and Mary Jones, Fonmon. An Arminian Methodist society probably met there. G. Williams, *Sheriffs of Glamorgan*, 67–8.

[2] By this time John Hodges had come under the influence of mysticism. One would infer from William Thomas, the diarist, that the Wenvoe society had died about 1755—possibly on the removal of Philip Thomas to Michaelston-le-Pit.

[3] Charles Wesley refers to 'our little society' at Aberthaw as early as 9 Sept. 1741. (Jackson, *Journal*, i. 298.) Mary Jones, Fonmon joined it once she moved to Ffontygari when her son Robert came of age.

I came to Chepstow WEDNESDAY the 31st just at noon
and began preaching immediately at Mr. Cheek's door.[1] The sun
shone full in my face, extremely hot, but in two or three minutes
the clouds covered it. The congregation was large and behaved
well; perhaps some may be *doers of the word*. When we went into
the boat at the Old Passage it was a dead calm, but the wind sprang
up in a few minutes so that we reached Bristol in good time.

XXIX

25 JULY–4 AUGUST 1764

Shrewsbury · Llanidloes · Pen-ffynnon · Ffair-rhos · Tregaron
Lampeter · Carmarthen · Pembroke · Haverfordwest
Pembroke · Laugharne · Llanstephan · Kidwelly · Oxwich
Cowbridge · Llandaf · Cardiff · Bristol

WEDNESDAY, 25 JULY 1764. I took horse [at Shrewsbury]
a little after four and, about twelve, preached in the market-house
at Llanidloes, two or three and forty miles from Shrewsbury. At
three we rode forward through the mountains to the *Fountain Head*.[2]
I was for lodging there but Mr. B.,[3] being quite unwilling, we
mounted again about seven. After having rode an hour, we found
we were quite out of the way, having been wrong directed at setting
out. We were then told to ride over some grounds, but our path
soon ended in the edge of a bog. However, we got through to a little
house where an honest man, instantly mounting his horse, galloped
before us, up hill and down, till he brought us into a road which, he
said, led straight to Ffair-rhos.[4] We rode on till another met us and

---

[1] The home of Moseley Cheek who, in 1765, became one of his Preachers.

[2] Pen-ffynnon (or Fountain Head), an inn at Cwmystwyth, between Rhaeadr and
Pont-rhyd-y-groes.

[3] Possibly T. Brisco—but there are no *Minutes of Conference* for 1763–4, while
those for 1765 give nine Preachers whose surname began with a B.

[4] Wesley wrote 'Roes-Fair', which Curnock interpreted as Rhos Fawr. But Rhos
Fawr is a farm on that same road which Wesley, in error, took to Aberystwyth. 'Roes-
fair' on the other hand (or Ffair-rhos, to give it its modern name) stood, and stands, on
his route from Cwmystwyth to the Abbey Farm near Strata Florida. The present Cross

said, 'No, this is the way to Aberystwyth. If you would go to Ffair-
rhos you must turn back and ride down to yonder bridge'. The
master of a little house near the bridge[1] then directed us to the next
village where we inquired again (it being past nine) and were once
more set exactly wrong. Having wandered an hour upon the mountains, through rocks and bogs and precipices, we with abundance of
difficulty got back to the little house near the bridge. It was in vain
to think of rest there, it being full of drunken, roaring miners;[2]
besides that there was but one bed in the house and neither grass
nor hay nor corn to be had. So we hired one of them to walk with
us to Ffair-rhos, though he was miserably drunk, till, by falling all
his length in a purling stream, he came tolerably to his senses.
Between eleven and twelve we came to the inn, but neither here
could we get any hay. When we were in bed the good hostler and
miner thought good to mount our beasts. I believe it was not long
before we rose that they put them into the stable. But the mule was
cut in several places, and my mare was bleeding like a pig from
a wound behind, two inches deep, made (it seemed) by a stroke with
a pitchfork. What to do we could not tell, till I remembered that
I had a letter for one Mr. Nathaniel Williams[3] whom, upon inquiry,
I found to live but a mile off. We walked thither and found *an
Israelite indeed*, who gladly received both man and beast.

After I had got a little rest, Mr. Williams desired me to give an
exhortation to a few of his neighbours. None was more struck there-
with than one of his own family who before cared for none of these
things. He sent a servant with us after dinner to Tregaron, from
whence we had a plain road to Lampeter.

Inn there, though old, has obviously been rebuilt, but according to the present owner
the only inn at Ffair-rhos has always stood on the same site.

[1] At Pont-rhyd-y-groes. The 'next village' was Ysbyty Ystwyth.

[2] These men worked in the local lead-mines. Then and later, many of them came
from Cornwall and brought their Methodism as well as their skill with them. Many of
their descendants became thoroughly Welsh, and not a few were to adorn the Methodist
ministry.

[3] The tenant of Mynachlog-fawr (or the Abbey farm), Strata Florida, who visited
Llangeitho to receive Holy Communion from Daniel Rowland. Both he and his brother
William (who owned extensive sheep runs from Tregaron to Abergwesyn) became
High Sheriffs of Cardiganshire in 1776 and 1751 respectively; Nathaniel was William's
heir and succeeded him at Pant-y-siri. *Bathafarn*, ii. 44; *J.H.S.P.C.W.* xxxi. 75;
S. R. Meyrick, *History and Antiquities of the County of Cardigan*, 336–7.

FRIDAY, 27. We rode through a lovely vale and over pleasant and fruitful hills to Carmarthen. Thence, after a short bait, we went on to Pembroke and came before I was expected. So I rested that night, having not quite recovered [from] my journey from Shrewsbury to Ffair-rhos.

SUNDAY, 29. The minister of St. Mary's[1] [Pembroke] sent me word he was very willing I should preach in his church, but before the service began the mayor sent to forbid it;[2] so he preached a very useful sermon himself. The mayor's behaviour so disgusted many of the gentry that they resolved to hear where they could, and accordingly flocked together in the evening from all parts of the town. And perhaps the taking up this cross may profit them more than my sermon in the church would have done.

MONDAY, 30. I rode to Haverfordwest, but no notice had been given, nor did any in the town know of my coming. However, after a short time I walked up towards the castle and began singing a hymn. The people presently ran together from all quarters. They have curiosity at least, and some, I cannot doubt, were moved by a nobler principle. Were zealous and active labourers here, what a harvest might there be, even in this corner of the land!

We returned through heavy rain to Pembroke.

TUESDAY, 31. We set out for Glamorgan[3] and rode up and down steep and stony mountains for about five hours to Laugharne. Having procured a pretty ready passage there, we went on to Llanstephan ferry where we were in some danger of being swallowed

---

[1] The Revd. David Lewis, *West Wales Historical Records*, iii. 232.

[2] Gwynne Davies, ibid. v. 124. On 11 Apr. 1764 Howell Harris and Nyberg, the Moravian, had spent the evening with John Barnes at Pembroke. 'There is a terrible confusion around Pembroke', wrote Nyberg later, 'between Barnes and the followers of Whitefield and Wesley' (*W.H.S. Proc.* xii. 46). The mayor's high-handed action, though quite illegal, is perhaps not altogether surprising against this background.

[3] From Nyberg's diary one also learns that Wesley dined 'at Esqr. Roch's at Clareston and said he once visited Hernhutt with satisfaction, but he thought the Brethren in England were somewhat fallen away'. M. H. Jones, who printed this extract in *W.H.S. Proc.* xii. 46 gave it under the date 30 July, but Mr. G. A. Dickman, the County Librarian of Pembrokeshire, who kindly looked it up for me, states that the correct date is 31 July. Clareston lies a little off the old Haverfordwest–Pembroke ferry road, and Richard Rodda is said to have been a steward there before becoming an Itinerant Preacher. Phillips, *History of Pembrokeshire*, 580.

up in the mud before we could reach the water. Between one and two we reached Kidwelly, having been more than seven hours on horseback, in which time we could have rode round by Carmarthen with more ease both to man and beast. I have therefore taken my leave of these ferries, considering we save no time by crossing them (not even when we have a ready passage) and so have all the trouble, danger and expense clear gains. I wonder that any man of common sense who has once made the experiment should ever ride from Pembroke to Swansea any other way than by Carmarthen.

An honest man at Kidwelly told us there was no difficulty in riding the sands, so we rode on. In ten minutes one overtook us who used to guide persons over them, and it was well he did, or in all probability we had been swallowed up. The whole sands are at least ten miles over, with many streams of quicksands intermixed. But our guide was thoroughly acquainted with them and with the road on the other side. By his help, between five and six, we came well tired to Oxwich in Gower.[1]

Gower is a large tract of land, bounded by Breconshire[2] on the north-east, the sea on the south-west and rivers on the other sides. Here all the people talk English and are in general the most plain, loving people in Wales. It is therefore no wonder that they receive the word with all readiness of mind.

Knowing that they were scattered up and down, I had sent two persons on Sunday, that they might be there early on Monday and so sent notice of my coming all over the country. But they came to Oxwich scarce a quarter of an hour before me, so that the poor people had no notice at all. Nor was there any to take us in, the person with whom the preacher used to lodge being three miles out of town.[3] After I had stayed a while in the street (for there was no

[1] On this tiring journey, Wesley probably crossed the old Pembroke ferry over the river Cleddau; rode through Burton to Clareston, then through Haverfordwest to Laugharne; crossed the river Taf by ferry from Laugharne to Black Scar; rode to Llanstephan; crossed the river Tywi by ferry to Ferryside; and then rode to Kidwelly. W. H. Morris in *Trinity Methodist Church, Kidwelly, 1866–1966*, 5, suggests that he then used the ford across the river Gwendraeth (about a quarter of a mile below the present bridge), followed a road across the marsh (now completely buried beneath silt) as far as Pen-bre and then crossed the Burry estuary.

[2] An obvious slip for Glamorgan.

[3] William Tucker of Horton, who later became leader of a society which met in his own home. The Oxwich society became the mother-church of Gower Methodism.

public house), a poor woman gave me house-room. Having had nothing since breakfast I was very willing to eat or drink, but she simply told me she had nothing in the house but a dram of gin. However, I afterwards procured a dish of tea at another house and was much refreshed. About seven I preached to a little company, and again in the morning. They were all attention, so that even for the sake of this handful of people I did not regret my labour.

WEDNESDAY, 1 AUGUST. It was with difficulty I reached Cowbridge about one, where the congregation was waiting. I found they had had heavy rain great part of the day, but very little fell upon us. Nor do I remember that from the beginning of March till now we have been in more than one heavy shower of rain, either in England, Scotland or Wales.

I preached in the evening at Llandaf, and on THURSDAY the 2nd in the Town Hall at Cardiff.

SATURDAY, 4. We crossed at the New Passage and rode on to Bristol.

XXX

29 AUGUST–12 SEPTEMBER 1767

Gloucester · Brecon · Carmarthen · Pembroke · Lamphey
Pembroke · Haverfordwest · St. Daniel's · Haverfordwest
Carmarthen · Swansea · Oxwich · Neath · Cowbridge
Cardiff · Llanbradach · Chepstow · Bristol

FRIDAY, 28 AUGUST 1767. I preached at Stow-on-the Wold about ten to a very dull, quiet congregation, and in the evening to almost such another at Gloucester.

SATURDAY, 29. We rode to Brecon.

SUNDAY, 30. One of Trefeca gave us a strange account. A young woman who served as a dairy-maid there was beloved by all the

Family. She was loving to everyone, never angry, never out of humour. That morning she was much happier, and had a fuller manifestation of the love of God, than ever. As she was coming through the entry a lad met her with a gun in his hand, which he did not know was charged. He presented it and said, 'Nanny, I will shoot you'. The gun went off and shot her through the heart. She fell on her face, and without any struggle or groan immediately expired.

I preached at eight to a large and serious congregation, and on the Bulwarks [at Brecon] at five.[1] A multitude of people attended and even the gentry seemed, for the present, *almost persuaded to be Christians.*

MONDAY, 31. I rode to Carmarthen and, a little before six, went down to the Green. The congregation was near as large as that at Brecon, but nothing so gay, being almost all poor or middling people. To these, therefore, I directly preached the gospel. They heard it with greediness and though I was faint and weary when I began, I was soon as a giant refreshed with wine.

TUESDAY, 1 SEPTEMBER. I rode on to Pembroke and, this and the next evening, preached in the main street to far more than the house could have contained. In the mornings we were within.

WEDNESDAY, 2. Upon inquiry I found the work of God in Pembrokeshire had been exceedingly hindered, chiefly by Mr. Davies' preachers,[2] who had continually inveighed against ours and thereby frighted abundance of people from hearing or coming near them. This had sometimes provoked them to retort, which always made a bad matter worse. The advice therefore which I gave them was

1. let all the people sacredly abstain from back-biting, tale-bearing, evil-speaking;

[1] Among his hearers was the young John Prickard (*post*, p. 96 n. 1.). *Arm. Mag.*, 1788, 460.
[2] 'Mr. Davies'—the Revd. Howell Davies, a Methodistical clergyman who deservedly earned the title 'the Apostle of Pembrokeshire'. He had little time for Wesley, however. *Ante*, p. xxxvi.

2. let all our preachers abstain from returning railing for railing, either in public or in private, as well as from disputing;

3. let them never preach controversy but plain, practical and experimental religion.

THURSDAY, 3. About noon I preached at Lamphey, a village two miles from Pembroke. The rain lessened the congregation but did not hinder the blessing. God was eminently present to comfort the mourners, as likewise at Pembroke in the evening.

SATURDAY, 5. I rode to Haverfordwest but knew not what to do because of the rain. However, at six I was constrained by the number of people to stand abroad, near the castle; and the whole congregation as quietly attended as if we had been in a cathedral.

SUNDAY, 6. I had a large and earnest congregation at six. About ten I began the service at St. Daniel's, a little church about half a mile from Pembroke which, till lately, lay in ruins.[1] It was thoroughly filled during the prayers and sermon, and a considerable number gladly partook of the Lord's Supper. Afterwards I rode back to Haverfordwest and, notwithstanding the rain, stood in the same place as before and applied *Oh that thou hadst known, at least in this thy day, the things that make for thy peace!*[2]

MONDAY, 7. I rode to Carmarthen and preached on the Green on *Is there no balm in Gilead?* In the afternoon, finding none that could direct us to Oxwich, we were obliged to ride round by Swansea. The next morning we came to Oxwich and found George Story[3]

---

[1] St. Daniel's, in the parish of St. Mary, which had been under the patronage of the Prior of St. Nicholas, Pembroke, was in ruins when Erasmus Saunders wrote his *View of the State of Religion in the Diocese of St. David's* in 1721; by Fenton's time it was a Methodist chapel—'a respectable building with stone tower and spire'. R. Fenton, *A Historical Tour through Pembrokeshire*, 206 (2nd edition). One of Howell Davies's four congregations met there as early as 1745. *West Wales Historical Records*, iii. 232; Saunders, op. cit. 24; *S.T.L.* (1742–47) 165 n. 6.

[2] On 10 Sept. Nyberg wrote in the Diary of the Moravian Congregation at Haverfordwest: 'Jn. Wesley preached this week three times in town, and strains hard to collect a Society. He told his few friends that they were welcome to hear the good Mr. Nyberg and also the good Mr. Howell Davies. Wesley was very kind indeed.' *W.H.S. Proc.* xii. 46–7.

[3] One of Wesley's Preachers, who had travelled on the 'Wales Circuit' the previous year.

there, who had come to Swansea the day before in his way to Cork. Hearing I was near, he came over just in season to preach to the congregation who waited for me. At noon I preached to, I suppose, all the inhabitants of the town and then rode to Neath.

I had designed to preach abroad, but the rain would not permit. The preaching-house was much crowded, and the power of God was in the midst of the congregation. Prejudices sunk down before it, and the innumerable lies which most of them had heard of me vanished into air. The same power rested upon them early in the morning. The bigots on all sides were ashamed and felt that, in Christ Jesus, nothing avails but the *faith that worketh by love.*

WEDNESDAY, 9. About twelve I preached to a large and serious congregation in the Assembly Room at Cowbridge, and in the evening in the court-house[1] at Cardiff where, both this and the following evening, we had most of the gentry in the town; and, both the mornings, the hearers were more than for many years. Who knows but, even in this desolate town, God may build up the waste places?

FRIDAY, 11. I rode to Llanbradach,[2] a single house, delightfully situated near the top of a high mountain, and in the evening preached to a serious company of plain Welshmen with uncommon enlargement of heart.

SATURDAY, 12. Setting out early, I reached Chepstow before noon and preached at a friend's door to a civil, unconcerned congregation. We came to the Old Passage (being told we had time to spare) a few minutes after the boat was gone off. Finding they would not pass again that day, I left my horses behind and, crossing over in a small boat, got to Bristol soon enough to preach in the evening.

[1] The Shire Hall.
[2] William Thomas of Llanbradach had married Mary, the eldest daughter of Robert and Mary Jones, Fonmon.

XXXI

1–13 AUGUST 1768

Shrewsbury · Strata Florida · Haverfordwest · Pembroke
St. Daniel's · Llanelli · Oxwich · Neath · Cowbridge · Cardiff
Llanbradach · Chepstow · Bristol

SUNDAY, 31 JULY 1768. I preached for Mr. Fletcher[1] in the morning, and in the evening at Shrewsbury.

MONDAY, 1 AUGUST. I lodged at the Abbey in Cardiganshire[2] and on Wednesday morning reached Haverfordwest. Here abundance of people flocked together and willingly *suffered the word of exhortation*. Indeed, a more quiet, humane, courteous people I have scarce ever seen. But I fear they were surfeited with preaching before we set foot in the town.[3]

SATURDAY, 6. I went to Pembroke. We were here several times before we had any place in Haverfordwest, but we have reason to fear lest the first become last.

SUNDAY, 7. I took a good deal of pains to compose the little misunderstandings which have much obstructed the work of God. At ten I read prayers, preached and administered the sacrament to a serious congregation at St. Daniel's. And the next morning left the people full of good desires and in tolerable good humour with each other.[4]

---

[1] The Revd. John Fletcher, vicar of Madeley in Shropshire—the 'saintly Fletcher of Madeley', a warm friend of John Wesley and for a short time President of Lady Huntingdon's College at Trefeca.

[2] No doubt with Nathaniel Williams.

[3] *Ante*, p. 65.

[4] Later in the month (on 29 Aug.) Nyberg told Howell Harris that John Wesley had been preaching a lot in Pembrokeshire recently. 'Our old friend John Wesley', he wrote, 'could not help throwing a fling at old harmless Gambold. I wish he would let us alone and preach Christ crucified' (M. H. Jones, *The Trevecka Letters*, 65; *S.T.L.* (*1747–94*), 126). John Gambold had been a member of the Holy Club at Oxford, had taken Holy Orders, and had then become a Moravian. In 1768 his health broke down and he returned to his native Pembrokeshire to take charge of the Moravian congregation at Haverfordwest.

MONDAY, 8. I rode to Llanelli and preached to a small, earnest company on *Ye are saved through faith.*[1] Thence we found a kind of way to Oxwich where I pressed the one thing needful on a plain, simple people, right willing to hear, with great enlargement of heart.

TUESDAY, 9. I took a full view of the castle, situated at the top of a steep hill and commanding a various and extensive prospect both by sea and land. The building itself is far the loftiest which I have seen in Wales.[2] What a taste had they who removed from hence to bury themselves in the hole at Margam!

When we came to Neath I was a little surprised to hear I was to preach in the church, of which the churchwardens had the disposal, the minister being just dead.[3] I began reading prayers at six but was greatly disgusted at the manner of singing:

1. twelve or fourteen persons kept it to themselves and quite shut out the congregation;

2. these repeated the same words, contrary to all sense and reason, six or eight or ten times over;

3. according to the shocking custom of modern music, different persons sung different words at one and the same moment, an intolerable insult on common sense and utterly incompatible with any devotion.

WEDNESDAY, 10. At five I had the pleasure of hearing the whole congregation at the room sing *with the spirit and the*

[1] Wesley was apparently invited to visit Llanelli by the two brothers Robert and John Deer. Hugh Hughes (who knew John Deer, junior, personally) in *Eurgrawn*, 1833, 89–90.

[2] Wesley was probably referring to Oxwich Castle (rather than to the ruins of the thirteenth-century Penrice castle on the other side of Oxwich Bay). It was a fortified manor-house built about the middle of the sixteenth century by Sir Rice Mansel, and was the home of Francis Bevan, an Oxwich Methodist who died on 8 Oct. 1840, aged 83, with whom Wesley stayed on later visits. (*W.M. Mag.*, 1841, 65.) It was inhabited (and by Bevans) within recent memory, but is now completely deserted and in the care of the Ministry of Public Buildings and Works. It commands a magnificent view over Oxwich Bay. The Mansels moved from Oxwich to Margam after buying Margam Abbey at the Dissolution, but Wesley would have been pleased to hear that within three years of his visit, Thomas Mansel Talbot began to build the elegant mansion known as Penrice Castle on the opposite hill and spent most of his time there.

[3] The Revd. Francis Pinkney, rector of Neath from 1737, died on 8 July 1768. Rayer MSS., f. 109.

understanding also; and again, at one in the afternoon at Cowbridge, where I found uncommon liberty of speech while I was explaining to many of the rich and gay, as well as to the poor, *The kingdom of God is within you*. I did not reach Cardiff till after seven where, finding the congregation waiting, I began immediately in the Town Hall, strongly exhorting them not to *receive the grace of God in vain*.

FRIDAY, 12. I preached at that lovely place Llanbradach; SATURDAY, the 13th, about noon at Chepstow. Thence I hastened to the Passage though everyone told me I had time enough and to spare. I had so, for I waited six hours, the boat being just gone when we came. About nine we got over and reached Bristol between eleven and twelve.

XXXII

25–7 JULY 1769

Dublin · Holyhead · Chester

MONDAY, 24 JULY 1769. After preaching in the evening [at Dublin] I went on board the packet[1] and the next afternoon landed at Holyhead. We reached Chester on THURSDAY morning. . . .

XXXIII

9–26 AUGUST 1769

Shrewsbury · Welshpool · Newtown · Tyddyn · Llanidloes
Strata Florida · Carmarthen · Haverfordwest · St. Daniel's
Pembroke · Haverfordwest · Carmarthen · Llanelli · Oxwich
Swansea · Neath · Bridgend · Cowbridge · Cardiff
Caerphilly · Llanbradach · Trefeca · Chepstow · Bristol

MONDAY, 7 AUGUST 1769. I returned to Manchester and on TUESDAY the 8th went on to Shrewsbury. I preached at

[1] The Trevor packet-boat. *W.H.S. Proc.* v. 75–8.

five and soon after, receiving an invitation from Mr. Powys at Berwick, I went over directly, gave a short exhortation, and returned to Salop.

WEDNESDAY, 9. We reached Welshpool before nine, where notice had been given of my preaching, the bailiff having granted the use of the Town Hall. But he had now changed his mind. So I rode on to Newtown and at one we went to the market-house. But in a few minutes a poor wretch, exceeding drunk, came in cursing and blaspheming and striking all that stood in his way. His stick was soon taken away from him, but the noise increasing, I removed to Bryn[1] and quietly finished my discourse.

At six in the evening I preached at Tyddyn,[2] the next morning at Llanidloes, and in the evening at the Abbey.[3]

FRIDAY, 11. I reached Carmarthen. The rain continuing, Mr. Peter Williams offered me his preaching-house,[4] in which I enforced *God forbid that I should glory save in the cross of our Lord Jesus Christ.*

SATURDAY, 12. I preached at Haverfordwest.

SUNDAY, 13. I went to St. Daniel's, and after reading prayers preached on those words in the Second Lesson, *What God hath cleansed, that call not thou common.* The bigots of all sides seemed

---

[1] A house about a mile to the north-west of Newtown, owned or tenanted by a Mr. Handcox (or Hardcox), whose housekeeper, Mrs. Corbett, gave Wesley some refreshment and became one of the first members of the Methodist society in Newtown. *Wes. Meth. Mag.*, 1836, 140–1.

[2] Tyddyn Gwyddfid, between Llanidloes and Llandinam, the home of Thomas Bowen, a Calvinistic Methodist exhorter whose sister Hannah was for many years matron of the Family at Trefeca (Roberts, *S.T.L.* (*1747–1794*) 26–8; *J.H.S.P.C.W.* viii. 57–62). Another sister, Sarah, married Simon Lloyd, Bala and their daughter Lydia married Thomas Foulks of Machynlleth, who retained his former membership of the English Wesleyan Methodist Society at Chester when he became a Welsh Calvinistic Methodist in Machynlleth. *D.W.B.*, s.n. Simon Lloyd and Thomas Foulks; *Bathafarn*, iv. 17–24; *Welsh. Wes. Meth.* 33–6.

[3] The Abbey farm, Strata Florida.

[4] The Revd. Peter Williams, a Methodistical clergyman and author of a well-known Biblical commentary. The preaching-house which he built for the Calvinistic Methodists of Carmarthen stood in Water Street. Gomer M. Roberts, *Bywyd a Gwaith Peter Williams*, 61.

ashamed before God, and I trust will not soon forget this day. In the afternoon I read prayers and preached again. I then met the society in Pembroke. Once more their little jars are laid asleep. God grant they may rise no more!

MONDAY, 14. I preached in the Town Hall to almost all the gentry in Pembroke, and I think, whatever they had before, they had then a clear call from God.

TUESDAY, 15. In the evening, although the wind was high, yet the largeness of the congregation obliged me to stand on the outside of the house at Haverfordwest.

WEDNESDAY, 16. I examined the members of the society, now the most lively one in Wales. Many of them are rejoicing in the love of God, and many groaning for full redemption.

Today I gave a second reading to that lively book, Mr. Newton's[1] account of his own experiences. There is something very extraordinary therein, but one may account for it without a jot of Predestination. I doubt not but his, as well as Colonel Gardiner's, conversion was an answer to his mother's prayers.

THURSDAY, 17. At twelve, I preached in the castle at Carmarthen, in the evening at Llanelli. The behaviour of Sir Thomas'[2] servants here (four or five of whom belong to the society) has removed all prejudice from him, as well as from most of the town. Indeed, they are a pattern to all of their rank, truly *adorning the doctrine of God our Saviour*.

FRIDAY, 18. I preached at eleven in Oxwich, and thence hastened to Swansea, where an effectual door is opened once more. The rain

---

[1] The Revd. John Newton, curate of Olney and later vicar of St. Mary Wolnooth, London, an evangelical clergyman, the author of some well-known hymns, and a supporter of William Wilberforce in his campaign against the slave trade.

[2] Sir Thomas Stepney (1725–72), 7th baronet, who lived at Llanelli House and whose wife Elizabeth was the daughter of Elizabeth Vaughan of Derllys and Thomas Lloyd, Trehir, and the niece of Madam Bridget Bevan (1698–1778). M. Clement in *Trans. Cymm.*, 1942, 75, and Francis Jones in ibid., 1964, 184–5. For the Stepneys *vide* Francis Green in *West Wales Historical Records*, vii. 108–42.

drove us into the room, which was hot as an oven, being much crowded both within and without.

SATURDAY, 19. About eight, I preached at Neath; about three in the church at Bridgend[1] (where the rain doubled the congregation by stopping the harvest-work); and at seven, in the Assembly Room at Cowbridge, on *Lord, are there few that be saved?* I was enabled to make a close and pointed application, I believe not without effect.

SUNDAY, 20. I preached there again at eight to a congregation who seemed to feel what was spoken. At eleven, the vicar[2] read prayers and I preached on those words in the Lesson, *Gallio cared for none of these things.* Most of the hearers seemed more awake than I expected, and a few appeared to be affected. In the evening, I took my old stand on the steps of the castle at Cardiff. Abundance of people were gathered together, it being a fair and mild evening, on whom I enforced *I saw the dead, small and great, stand before God.*

TUESDAY, 22. Mr. Davies[3] read the prayers, and I preached, in Caerphilly church, and in the evening at Llanbradach.

WEDNESDAY, 23. I went on to Trefeca. Here we found a concourse of people from all parts of Wales, come to celebrate the Countess of Huntingdon's birthday and the anniversary of her school, which was opened on August 24 of last year. I preached in

---

[1] St. Mary's, Nolton.

[2] Revd. William Miles, vicar of Llanblethian-cum-Cowbridge, 1748–73. L. J. Hopkin-James, op. cit. 203–4.

[3] Not the Revd. Howell Davies (as in Curnock, v. 333 n. 4) but the Revd. Thomas Davies (1753–1819), a native of Talley, Carmarthenshire, curate of Llan-gors and Cathedine (1766–9) and rector of Coety (1769–1819). The livings of Coety, Coychurch, and Llan-gan (all within a few miles of each other) were in the patronage of the Methodistical Lady Charlotte Edwin, daughter of the 4th Duke of Hamilton and the wife of Charles Edwin, M.P. for Glamorgan 1747–56. Thomas Davies, like Edward Davies, Coychurch, and David Jones, Llan-gan, was a Methodistical clergyman. He frequently visited Trefeca, and during his absence David Jones often supplied his pulpit at Coety, just as he supplied Llan-gan during David Jones's absence in England assisting Lady Huntingdon. He seems to have had a high opinion of Wesley (Howell Harris noted on the previous 15 July that he was 'all Wesley'), and doubtless accompanied him on this journey via Cardiff and Caerphilly. *J.H.S.P.C.W.* xlvi. 1–16, 36–45; Beynon, *Howell Harris, Reformer and Soldier*, 226.

the evening to as many as her chapel could well contain, which is extremely neat—or rather elegant—as is the dining room, the school, and all the house. About nine, Howell Harris desired me to give a short exhortation to his Family. I did so, and then went back to my Lady's, and laid me down in peace.

THURSDAY, 24. I administered the Lord's Supper to the Family.[1] At ten, the public service began [in the College]. Mr. Fletcher preached an exceeding lively sermon in the court, the chapel being far too small. After him Mr. William Williams preached in Welsh till between one and two o'clock. At two we dined. Meantime, a large number of people had baskets of bread and meat carried to them in the court. At three I took my turn there, then Mr. Fletcher and, about five, the congregation was dismissed. Between seven and eight the lovefeast began, at which I believe many were comforted. In the evening several of us retired into the neighbouring wood, which is exceeding pleasantly laid out in walks, one of which leads to a little mount, raised in the midst of a meadow, that commands a delightful prospect. This is Howell Harris' work, who has likewise greatly enlarged and beautified his house, so that, with the gardens, orchards, walks and pieces of water that surround it, it is a kind of little paradise.

FRIDAY, 25. We rode through a lovely country to Chepstow.[2] I had designed to go straight on, but yielded to the importunity of our friends to stay and preach in the evening. Meantime, I took a walk through Mr. Morris' woods.[3] There is scarce anything like

---

[1] But according to Seymour, *The Life of . . . Countess of Huntingdon*, ii. 99, to the clergymen, then the students, and then to Lady Huntingdon's party at the College (now known as the College Farm, but formerly Trefeca Isaf). John Wesley had never been enamoured of the College from the start and was not present when it was opened in 1768, but his brother Charles administered the sacrament there the following month. On this visit in 1769 John was accompanied by Moseley Cheek and probably Henry Lloyd. *Itinerary*, 11 Sept. 1768 and 24 Aug. 1769.

[2] Through the delightful vale of Usk.

[3] Valentine Morris, junr. (1727–89) of Piercefield, an estate overlooking the Wye near the Chepstow–Monmouth road. Helped by his wife, he so improved it that it became almost legendary for its beauty; Arthur Young, for example, thought it exceeded anything of the kind he had ever seen. But Morris, though extremely generous and hospitable (he allowed conducted tours of the grounds twice a week) was extravagant, ostentatious, and an inveterate gambler, with the result that he was obliged to convey

them in the kingdom. They stand on the top and down the side of a steep mountain, hanging in a semi-circular form over the river. Through these woods abundance of serpentine walks are cut, wherein many seats and alcoves are placed, most of which command a surprising prospect of rocks and fields on the other side of the river. And must all these be burned up? What will become of us then, if we set our hearts upon them?

SATURDAY, 26. Resolving not to be too late now, as I was last year, I took horse at four, but being earnestly engaged in conversation, we missed our way and came to the Passage just as the boat was gone. About three in the afternoon it passed again, and soon after six we reached Bristol.

XXXIV

12–31 AUGUST 1771

Bristol · Chepstow · Brecon · Hay · Brecon · Carmarthen
Haverfordwest · Dale · Houghton · Pembroke · St. Daniel's
Llanelli · Oxwich · Swansea · Neath · Coychurch · Cowbridge
Cardiff · Bristol

MONDAY, 12 AUGUST 1771. I set out for Wales and, after preaching at Chepstow and Brecon, on WEDNESDAY the 14th came to Hay. Here I met with Dr. Maclaine's translation of Mosheim's *Ecclesiastical History*.[1] Certainly he is a very sensible translator of a very sensible writer, but I dare not affirm that either one or the other was acquainted with inward religion. The translator mentions, without any blame, Mr. Stinstra's 'Letter against Fanaticism' which, if the reasoning were just, would fix the charge of fanaticism on our Lord Himself and all His apostles. In[2] truth

Piercefield in 1772 to trustees and to live on his property in the West Indies. A portion of the park is now Chepstow Racecourse. Ivor Waters, *The Unfortunate Valentine Morris, passim,* and in *Presenting Monmouthshire,* No. 14, 30–8; Bradney, *A History of Monmouthshire,* iv, Part I, 36–9.

[1] Dr. A. Maclaine's translation of Mosheim's work had appeared in 1764.

[2] John Stinstra was an Anabaptist minister in Friesland who published his pastoral letter in 1752. Curnock, v. 426 n. 3.

I cannot but fear Mr. Stinstra is in the same class with Dr. Conyers Middleton,[1] and aims every blow, though he seems to look another way, at the fanatics who wrote the Bible. The very thing which Mr. Stinstra calls fanaticism is no other than heart-religion; in other words, *righteousness and peace and joy in the Holy Ghost*. These must be *felt*, or they have no being. All therefore who condemn inward feelings in the gross leave no place either for joy, peace or love in religion and consequently reduce it to a dry, dead carcase.

In the evening I preached in the new neat preaching-house to many more than it would contain. The next evening I was constrained to preach abroad.

FRIDAY, 16. I returned to Brecon and after spending two comfortable days there, on MONDAY the 19th rode to Carmarthen. The rain obliged me to preach within.

TUESDAY, 20. I rode to Haverfordwest and in the evening preached in St. Martin's churchyard to a numerous and deeply attentive congregation. The next evening I strongly applied the story of Dives and Lazarus, and many were almost persuaded to be Christians.

I rode on THURSDAY the 22nd to Dale, a little village at the mouth of Milford Haven. It seemed to me that our preachers had bestowed here much pains to little purpose. The people, one and all, seemed as dead as stones—perfectly quiet and perfectly unconcerned. I told them just what I thought. It went as a sword to their hearts. They *felt* the truth and wept bitterly. I know not where we have found more of the presence of God. Shall we at last have fruit here also?

FRIDAY, 23. I preached at noon to a lovely congregation of plain, artless people at Houghton, and in the Town Hall at Pembroke in the evening to many rich and elegant hearers.

[1] Dr. Conyers Middleton had published in 1749 a work in which he had denounced the practice of accepting the primitive fathers as exponents of the Christian faith. Wesley had written a reply to it, running to 102 pages, under the title *A Letter to the Rev. Dr. Conyers Middleton, occasioned by his late 'Free Inquiry'*. Tyerman, *Wesley*, ii. 34, 61-2.

SUNDAY, 25 At ten I began the service at St. Daniel's. The church, as usual, would ill contain the congregation. In the afternoon I preached in Monkton Priory church (one of three belonging to Pembroke), a large, old ruinous building.[1] I suppose it has scarce had such a congregation in it during this century. Many of them were gay, genteel people, so I spake on the first elements of the Gospel. But I was still out of their depth. Oh! how hard it is to be shallow enough for a polite audience!

MONDAY, 26. I rode to Llanelli and, at six, read prayers and preached in another large church,[2] almost as ruinous as that at Pembroke. The congregation was numerous, yet most of them seemed to understand what they heard.

TUESDAY, 27. We crept through a right Welsh road, and reached Oxwich between twelve and one. The congregation had waited for some time, so I began without delay. The road to Swansea was a little better, so I reached the town in time, and, at six, preached in the yard, as our room would contain hardly a third of the people.

WEDNESDAY, 28. I called at Neath on one of our friends, but before I could sit down, was informed a congregation was waiting for me. This I had no thought of. However, I gave them a short sermon, and hastened on to Coychurch, near Bridgend.[3] I preached as deliberately as possible, as great part of the audience were Welsh, and I believe, by this means, all of them could understand at least the substance of the discourse. About six, I preached in the Town

---

[1] St. Nicholas church, Monkton stood originally within Pembroke Castle but was later removed to Monkton. The presentation to the church was vested in the priory of St. Nicholas before the Dissolution. From 1770 to 1790 the same person—the Revd. George Seall—held the three livings of St. Michael's, St. Mary's, and St. Nicholas; indeed, the three went together until 1872. *West Wales Historical Records*, iii. 232–6.

[2] St. Elli's church. Revd. Theophilus Davies was vicar, 1761–87.

[3] The incumbent of Coychurch from 1768 until his death in 1812 was the Revd. Edward Davies. But as he was not fluent in Welsh, and enjoyed only indifferent health, he accepted a curacy at Batheaston in 1789 and thereafter resided only occasionally at Coychurch. Prior to his coming to Wales, he held the living of Bengeworth near Evesham, and on 17 Mar. 1768 he invited John Wesley to preach in his church. His curate at Coychurch from 1742 until 1779 was Thomas Richards, the lexicographer. *J.H.S.P.C.W.* xlvi. 69–72.

Hall at Cowbridge to high and low, rich and poor, and the two next evenings in the court-house[1] at Cardiff, to a still larger congregation. Afterwards, we had a comfortable lovefeast, which brought to our mind former days, when we praised God with Ann Jenkins, Arthur Price and Thomas Glascott, before Thomas Prosser sowed the deadly tares among them.

SATURDAY, 31. I returned to Bristol.

XXXV

12–29 AUGUST 1772

Shrewsbury · Hay · Trefeca · Brecon · Carmarthen Haverfordwest · Llwyngwair · Newport · Haverfordwest Pembroke · St. Daniel's · Haverfordwest · Llanelli · Swansea Bridgend · Cowbridge · Cardiff · Caerphilly · Bristol

WEDNESDAY, 12 AUGUST 1772. I preached at Salop and spake strong words, to the amazement of many notional believers.

THURSDAY, 13. I preached at Hay.

FRIDAY, 14. About noon, at the request of my old friend Howell Harris, I preached at Trefeca on *the strait gate*. And we found our hearts knit together as at the beginning. He said, 'I have borne with those pert, ignorant young men, vulgarly called students, till I cannot in conscience bear any longer. They preach bare-faced Reprobation and so broad Antinomianism that I have been constrained to oppose them to the face, even in the public congregation'. It is no wonder they should preach thus. What better can be expected from raw lads of little understanding, little learning, and no experience?

After spending a day or two very comfortably at Brecon, on MONDAY the 17th I preached in the castle at Carmarthen, and

[1] i.e. in the Shire Hall.

on TUESDAY the 18th in the new house at Haverfordwest,[1] far the neatest in Wales. There is a considerable increase in this society, and not in number only. After preaching on WEDNES-DAY evening we had such a meeting as I have seldom known. Almost everyone spoke, as well as they could for tears, and with the utmost simplicity. And many of them appeared to know *the great salvation*, to love God with all their hearts.

THURSDAY, 20. I rode over to Mr. Bowen's at Llwyn-gwair, an agreeable place and an agreeable family.[2] Here I rejoiced to meet with Mr. Pugh, whose living is within a mile of Llwyn-gwair.[3] In the evening he read prayers at Newport and preached to a deeply serious congregation. I trust his lot is cast for good among a people both desirous and capable of instruction.

FRIDAY, 21. I preached again about eight and then rode back to Haverfordwest. After dinner we hasted to the passage, but the watermen were not in haste to fetch us over so I sat down on a convenient stone and finished the little tract I had in hand.[4] However, I got to Pembroke in time and preached in the Town Hall, where we had a solemn and comfortable opportunity.

[1] A plain building adjacent to St. Mary's church, opened in 1772 and known for many years as 'the Wesley room'. J. Ivor John, *Wesley Methodist Church, Haverfordwest, 1763–1963*, 16; *Arm. Mag.*, 1795, 267; J. Brown, *A History of Haverfordwest . . .*, 78.

[2] A certain George Williams, who may have been a member of the Pembroke society but who is otherwise unknown, had informed Wesley on the previous 23 July that George Bowen of Llwyn-gwair (who had contributed handsomely towards the cost of the new meeting-house at Haverfordwest) was anxious to meet him at his house; hence this visit, the first of six. Bowen was very well disposed towards the Welsh Methodists (one of his daughters married the Revd. David Griffiths, the Methodistical rector of Nevern), and he was largely instrumental in resuscitating the Circulating Schools in 1805. *Vide* a full account (in Welsh) of the family by W. Islwyn Morgan in *Bathafarn*, xxii. 37–47 and xxiii. 14–24.

[3] The Revd. David Pugh, the Methodistical rector of Newport, Pembs. who was one of those Evangelicals who joined Thomas Haweis's society at Oxford *c.* 1758 and who, as a clergyman, sympathized with the Moravians, the Welsh Methodists, Lady Huntingdon's preachers, and John Wesley. He strongly opposed the proposal to ordain Welsh Calvinistic laymen in 1811. *J.H.S.P.C.W.* xxxix. 34–7.

[4] Possibly his reply to Richard Hill's attacks upon him, which he published under the title: *Some Remarks on Mr. Hill's 'Review of all the Doctrines taught by Mr. John Wesley'*. Tyerman, *Wesley*, iii. 138, 143.

SUNDAY, 23. The violent rain considerably lessened our congregation at St. Daniel's.[1] Afterwards the wind was so extremely high that I doubted if we could cross the passage. But it stood exactly in the right point, and we got to Haverfordwest just before the thunder-storm began. In the evening I took my leave of this loving people and the next day reached Llanelli.

TUESDAY, 25. I went on to Swansea and preached in the evening to a numerous congregation. I preached in Oldcastle church, near Bridgend, about noon on WEDNESDAY the 26th and in the evening in the Assembly Room at Cowbridge to an unusually serious congregation.

THURSDAY, 27. I preached at Cardiff in the Town Hall, as also the following evening; about noon in the little church at Caerphilly.

SATURDAY, 29. I went on to Bristol.

XXXVI

15–27 AUGUST 1774

Bristol · Cardiff · Llandaff · Cowbridge · Swansea · Llanelli
Laugharne · Pembroke · St. Daniel's · Haverfordwest
New Inn · Brecon · Hay · Bristol

MONDAY, 15 AUGUST 1774. I set out [from Bristol] for Wales but did not reach Cardiff till near eight o'clock. As the congregation was waiting in the Town Hall, I went thither without delay and many, I believe, did not regret the time they had waited there.

[1] Curnock was mistaken when he stated (op. cit. v. 483 n. 3) that the vicar of St. Daniel's was John Wesley, A.M. No person of this famous name held a living in Pembrokeshire at this time. Probably *the* John Wesley signed the register at some time or other, and this may have misled Curnock.

TUESDAY, 16. I preached about noon in the great hall at Llan-daf[1] on *It is appointed unto men once to die.* Strange doctrine, and not very welcome to the inhabitants of palaces!

WEDNESDAY, 17. At eleven I preached in the Town Hall at Cowbridge, the neatest place of the kind I have ever seen.[2] Not only the floor, the walls, the ceiling are kept exactly clean but every pane of glass in the windows.

Hence I hastened on to Swansea, and at seven preached in the castle to a large congregation. The next morning I went on to Llanelli, but what a change was there! Sir Thomas Stepney, the father of the poor, was dead, cut down in the strength of his years! So the family was broke up and Wilfred Colley, his butler, the father of the society, obliged to remove.[3] Soon after, John Deer, who was next in usefulness to him, was taken into Abraham's bosom. But just then, Col. St. Leger, in the neighbourhood, sent to Galway for Lieutenant Cook to come and put his house into repair and manage his estate.[4] So another is brought, just in time to supply the place of Wilfred Colley![5] I preached at five near Sister Deer's door to a good company of plain country people, and then rode over to the old ruinous house which Mr. Cook is making all haste to repair. It is not unlike old Mr. Gwynne's house at Garth, having a few

[1] At Llandaf Court, the home of Thomas Mathews.

[2] The Town Hall at Cowbridge had been repaired in 1768, and was to be repaired again in 1778. L. J. Hopkin-James, *Old Cowbridge*, 55, 57.

[3] Wilfred Colley moved to Cardiff where he was a shopkeeper. His name appears among those who attended a vestry meeting of St. John's church in 1777, and it was he 'and others' who paid the rates for the meeting-house in Church Street the following year. J. H. Matthews, *Cardiff Records*, iii. 476, 488.

[4] The evidence adduced by W. Kemmis Buckley in *Bathafarn*, xxv. 35–7 seems to be conclusive: Col. St. Leger lived at Plas Trimsaran. The Colonel married Lady Mary Mansel, widow of Sir Edward Mansel of Plas Trimsaran and Strade. As Sir Edward died without issue in 1754 and dispossessed his nephew and heir (Sir Edward Vaughan Mansel) of the Trimsaran property, the latter succeeded only to Strade; Plas Trimsaran then passed to the widow and her second husband, Col. Barry St. Leger. Wesley had met Lieut. Cook (who fought under Wolfe in Canada) in Galway on 6 June 1765. Curnock, v. 129–30.

[5] The effective leader of the Llanelli society after John Deer's death was Henry Child, father-in-law of the Revd. James Buckley, a prominent and very successful Preacher in Wales (and Methodism generally) in the late eighteenth and early nineteenth centuries. *Vide* W. Kemmis Buckley in *Bathafarn*, xxv. 28–35. Curnock (op. cit. vi. 36, n. 2) confused the Arminian John Deer of Llanelli with the Calvinist John Deer of St. Nicholas in Glamorgan.

large, handsome rooms. It is also situated much like that, only not quite so low, for it has the command of a well-cultivated vale and of the fruitful side of the opposite mountain.

FRIDAY, 19. We rode on to Laugharne ferry and, seeing a person just riding over the ford, we followed him with ease, the water scarce reaching above our horses' knees. Between two and three, we came to Pembroke.

SUNDAY, 21. At nine, I began the service at St. Daniel's, and concluded a little before twelve. It was a good time. The power of the Lord was unusually present, both to wound and to heal. Many were constrained to cry, while others were filled with speechless awe and silent love.

After dinner, I went over to Haverfordwest, but could not preach abroad because of the rain. Both here and at Pembroke I found the people in general to be in a cold, dead, languid state. And no wonder, since there has been for several months a total neglect of discipline. I did all I could to awaken them once more, and left them full of good resolutions.[1]

TUESDAY, 23. I went to the New Inn near Llandeilo, and on WEDNESDAY the 24th to Brecon. In the evening I preached in the Town Hall to most of the gentry in the town. They behaved well, though I used great plainness of speech in describing *the narrow way.*

THURSDAY, 25. At eleven I preached within the walls of the old church at Hay. Here and everywhere I heard the same account of the proceedings at Llan-crwys.[2] The Jumpers (all who were there informed me) were first in the court and afterwards in the house. Some of them leaped up many times, men and women, several feet

---

[1] The two Preachers on the Pembrokeshire Circuit in 1773–4 were Richard Whatcoat and Charles Boon.

[2] Curnock inserted '[Llancroyes]'; Wesley, in the first edition of his Journal, omitted the name entirely. It is difficult to understand why Llan-crwys, which had been so much in the news in 1763, should still be a talking-point in 1774; such physical manifestations were not confined to this Carmarthenshire parish. Moreover, in the above context, somewhere much nearer Hay is surely implied.

from the ground. They clapped their hands with the utmost violence; they shook their heads; they distorted all their features; they threw their arms and legs to and fro in all variety of postures; they sung, roared, shouted, screamed with all their might to the no small terror of those that were near them. One gentlewoman told me she had not been herself since and did not know when she should. Meantime, the person of the house was delighted above measure and said, 'Now the power of God is come indeed!'.

SATURDAY, 27. Being detained some hours at the Old Passage, I preached to a small congregation and in the evening returned to Bristol.

XXXVII

16–28 AUGUST 1775

London · Trefeca · Brecon · Carmarthen · Pembrokeshire
Carmarthenshire · Cardiff · Newport · New Passage

MONDAY, 14 AUGUST 1775. Having spent a few days in town, on Monday the 14th I set out for Wales, and WEDNES-DAY the 16th reached Hay. Being desired to give them one sermon at Trefeca I turned aside thither and on THURSDAY the 17th preached at eleven to a numerous congregation. What a lovely place! And what a lovely Family! Still consisting of about six score persons. So the good *man is turned again to his dust*. But *his thoughts do not perish*.[1]

I preached at Brecon[2] the next day and on SATURDAY the 19th went to Carmarthen. How is the wilderness become a fruitful field! A year ago I knew no one in this town who had any desire of fleeing from the wrath to come, and now we have eighty persons

[1] Howell Harris had died on 21 July 1773.
[2] Samuel Bradburn, on his way to his new circuit in Pembrokeshire, unexpectedly met Wesley at Brecon and heard him preach at Brecon, Carmarthen, Haverfordwest and Pembroke. *Memorandum Book*, i, Aug. 1775.

in society.¹ It is true not many of them are awakened, but they have broke off their outward sins. Now let us try whether it be not possible to prevent the greater part of these from drawing back. . . .²

. . . After making a little tour through Carmarthenshire, Pembrokeshire and Glamorgan, on MONDAY the 28th, setting out early from Cardiff, I reached Newport about eight and soon after preached to a large congregation. I believe it is five-and-thirty years since I preached here before, to a people who were then wild as bears. How amazingly is the scene changed! O! what is too hard for God!

We came to the New Passage just as the boat was putting off, so I went in immediately. Some friends were waiting for me on the other side, who received me as one risen from the dead.³

XXXVIII

9–28 JULY 1777

*Malvern · Monmouth · Brecon · Garth (?) · Llandeilo
Carmarthen · Llwyn-gwair · Newport · Cardigan · Newport
Trecwn · Haverfordwest · Roch · Haverfordwest · Houghton
Pembroke · St. Daniel's · Jeffreston · Carmarthen · Llanelli
Swansea · Neath · Margam · Bridgend · Cowbridge
Llantwit Major · Ffontygari · Fonmon · Penmark · Cardiff
Caerphilly · Llandaf · Newport · Bristol*

WEDNESDAY, 9 JULY 1777. I went through a delightful vale to Malvern, lying on the side of a high mountain, and

¹ Charles Boon, one of the Preachers on the Glamorgan Circuit in 1774–5, preached in the Moravian room at Carmarthen on the invitation of one Lazarus Thomas, and Thomas and four or five other Moravians became Methodists late in November or early in December 1774 (*J.H.S.P.C.W.* xxi. 61–3). This was probably the origin of the Wesleyan society at Carmarthen which, a month after Wesley's visit, numbered over 100 members. Bradburn, op. cit., 12 Sept. 1775.

² At this point in his Journal, Wesley inserted a lengthy letter which he had received from one of his Preachers at West Bromwich; hence probably the brevity of his account of this visit to South Wales.

³ From a loose sheet of paper in the Dowlais Collection (D/DG 369) in the Glamorgan County Record Office (which may have belonged originally to the Brecon Circuit Book), Wesley was accompanied on a part of this visit by John Broadbent, who was probably on his way to his new circuit in Pembrokeshire.

commanding one of the finest prospects in the world—the whole Vale of Evesham. Hitherto, the roads were remarkably good, but they grew worse till we came to Monmouth. Much disturbance was expected here, but we had none; all were deeply attentive.[1]

About six in the evening, on THURSDAY the 10th, I preached on the Bulwarks at Brecon.

FRIDAY, 11. I called upon Mr. Gwynne, just recovering from a dangerous illness, but he is not recovered from the seriousness which it occasioned. May this be a lasting blessing![2]

SATURDAY, 12. We dined at Llandeilo. After dinner, we walked in Mr. Rice's park, one of the pleasantest I ever saw; it is so finely watered by the winding river running through and round the gently rising hills.[3] Near one side of it, on the top of a high eminence, is the old castle, a venerable pile at least as old as William the Conqueror and 'majestic though in ruins'.

In the evening I preached to a large congregation in the market-place at Carmarthen. I was afterwards informed the mayor had sent two constables to forbid my preaching there, but if he did their hearts failed them for they said not one word.

SUNDAY, 13. We had a plain, useful sermon from the vicar,[4] though some said 'He did not preach the gospel'. He preached what

[1] The Wesleyan Methodists of Monmouth probably experienced more bitter and prolonged persecution than any in Wales.

[2] Marmaduke Gwynne, the Methodist, died in 1769. He was succeeded by his heir Howell Gwynne who, in 1769, moved to Llanelwedd Hall, near Builth, and handed Garth over to *his* heir, another Marmaduke. If, therefore, Wesley called at Llanelwedd, he was referring to Howell Gwynne, but if at Garth the reference is to Marmaduke, his son. In his later years Marmaduke's health deteriorated, and he died in London in 1784; his father died in 1780. I have discussed the Gwynne genealogy in *Brycheiniog*, xiv. 79-96, and the Methodist's relations with Howell Harris in *J.H.S.P.C.W.* lv. 65-81, and with his chaplain, the Revd. Theophilus Evans, in *N.L.W. Journal*, xvi. 264-71.

[3] Dynevor, the seat of George Rice (1724-79), a descendant of Gruffydd ap Nicholas (*fl.* 1425-56). He played a very prominent part in the political life of Carmarthenshire and represented the county in Parliament from 1754 to 1779. *D.W.B.*, s.n. Though Dynevor (or Dinefwr) was an ancient stronghold of the native rulers of Deheubarth, the 'majestic ruin' which Wesley saw was built *c.* 1200, and enlarged later, especially in the late thirteenth century.

[4] The Revd. John Rogers, vicar of St. Peter's, Carmarthen 1752-96. *Trans. Carms. Ant. Soc.* iii. 42; iv. 30.

these men have great need to hear lest they seek death in the error of their life. In the evening I explained to a huge congregation who it is that builds his house upon a rock. I believe many had ears to hear, even of the young and gay, to whom I made a particular application.

MONDAY, 14. I reached Llwyn-gwair about noon. In the evening Mr. Pugh read prayers and I preached at Newport. This is the only town in Wales which I had then observed to increase. In riding along on the side of Newport bay I observed on the ground a large quantity of turfs. These are found by removing the sand above high-water mark, under which there is a continued bed of turf with the roots of trees, leaves, nuts and various kinds of vegetables. So that it is plain the sea is an intruder here and now covers what was once dry land. Such probably was the whole bay a few centuries ago. Nay, it is not at all improbable that formerly it was dry land from Aberystwyth to St. David's Point.[1]

TUESDAY, 15. Mr. Bowen carried me in his chaise to Cardigan. This is the second town I have seen in Wales which is continually increasing both in buildings and in number of inhabitants. I preached at noon, five or six clergymen being present with a numerous congregation, and a more attentive one I have not seen. Many likewise appeared deeply affected. If our preachers constantly attended here I cannot think their labour would be in vain.

WEDNESDAY, 16. About nine I preached again in Newport church and found much liberty among that poor simple people. We dined with Admiral Vaughan at Trecwn, one of the most delightful spots that can be imagined.[2] Thence we rode to Haverfordwest, but the heat and dust were as much as I could bear. I was

---

[1] Wesley was perfectly correct; the story of 'Cantre'r Gwaelod'—the buried 'city' beneath the sea—is one of the best-known of Welsh legends.

[2] John Vaughan, Admiral (Blue) in 1787 died two years later, unmarried; on the death of his sister Martha in 1803 the family name of Vaughan became extinct at Trecwn, but a descendant founded the Barham Memorial School in the village in 1875 and transferred it to the Methodist Education Committee. *W.H.S. Proc.* xi. 23–4; *Bathafarn*, iii. 27–35. One of the Admiral's sisters was a member of the Haverfordwest society.

faint for a while, but it was all gone as soon as I came into the congregation, and after preaching and meeting the society I was as fresh as at six in the morning.

THURSDAY, 17. I preached at Roch and took a view of the old castle, built on a steep rock. A gentleman wisely asked Mr. S:[1] 'Pray, is this natural or artificial?'. He gravely replied: 'Artificial to be sure; I imported it from the north of Ireland'.

FRIDAY, 18. The more I converse with the society at Haverford-west the more I am united to them.

SATURDAY, 19. About eleven I preached at Houghton, two miles short of the ferry. There was an uncommon blessing among the simple-hearted people. At Pembroke in the evening we had the most elegant congregation I have seen since we came into Wales. Some of them came in dancing and laughing as into a theatre, but their mood was quickly changed and in a few minutes they were as serious as my subject—Death. I believe, if they do not take great care, they will remember it—for a week!

SUNDAY, 20. The congregation at St. Daniel's was more than the church could contain. After reading prayers, I preached an hour (an uncommon thing with me) on *Not everyone that saith unto Me 'Lord, Lord'*. Many were cut to the heart, and at the Lord's Supper many were wounded and many healed. Surely now, at least, if they do not harden their hearts, all these will know the day of their visitation.

MONDAY, 21. Having been much pressed to preach at Jeffreston, a colliery, six or seven miles from Pembroke, I began soon after seven. The house was presently filled and all the space about the doors and windows, and the poor people drank in every word. I had finished my sermon when a gentleman, violently pressing in, bade the people get home and mind their business. As he used some bad words my driver spake to him. He fiercely said, 'Do you think

---

[1] John Rees Stokes of Cuffern, near Roch, whose wife Frances was the sister of Catherine (or Kitty) Warren of Haverfordwest. Phillips, *History of Pembrokeshire*, 579.

need to be taught by a chaise-boy?'. The lad replying, 'Really, sir, I do think so', the conversation ended.

In the evening I preached in the market-place at Carmarthen to such another congregation as I had there before, and my heart was so enlarged towards them that I continued preaching a full hour.

TUESDAY, 22. I preached at Llanelli about one, and at Swansea in the evening.

WEDNESDAY, 23. I preached in Swansea at five, in Neath between eight and nine, and about one at Margam. In the road between this and Bridgend we had the heaviest rain I ever remember to have seen in Europe. And it saved John Prickard's[1] life, for presently man and beast were covered with a sheet of lightning; but as he was thoroughly wet, it did him no harm. In the evening, I preached in Oldcastle church near Bridgend.

THURSDAY, 24. I preached to a large and serious congregation in the Town Hall at Cowbridge.

FRIDAY, 25. About eleven, I read prayers and preached in Llantwit Major church to a very numerous congregation. I have not seen either so large or so handsome a church since I left England. It was sixty yards long, but one end of it is now in ruins. I suppose it has been abundantly the most beautiful as well as the most spacious church in Wales.[2]

In the evening, I preached at Mrs. Jones' house in Ffontygari.[3] For the present, even the genteel hearers seemed affected, and God is able to continue the impression.

SATURDAY, 26. I breakfasted at Fonmon castle, and found a melancholy pleasure in the remembrance of past time. About noon,

[1] John Prickard, a native of Pembrokeshire but brought up by his uncle at Brecon He became an Itinerant Preacher, and when he died in 1784 he was described in the *Minutes of Conference* as 'an eminent pattern of holiness'.
[2] Apart from the 'Westley' memorial tablets in Llantwit Major church, a local tradition still persists, it is alleged, that a branch of the Wesley family lived at Leechmore, some three miles to the north-west. S. Awbery in *Vale of History* (ed. by Stewart Williams), 64; Richard Butterworth in *W.H.S. Proc.* iii. 131–2.
[3] Now the Country Club.

I preached at Penmark,[1] and in the evening in that memorable old castle at Cardiff.

SUNDAY, 27. I preached in the Town Hall, and again in the afternoon to a crowded audience, after preaching in a little church at Caerphilly.[2] In the evening I preached in Mr. M's[3] hall at Llandaf, and God applied His word (I think) to every heart.

MONDAY, 28. I preached at Newport, and in the evening reached Bristol.

XXXIX

29 SEPTEMBER–2 OCTOBER 1777

Bristol · Llwyn-gwair · Fishguard · Dublin

SATURDAY, 27 SEPTEMBER 1777. Having abundance of letters from Dublin informing me that the society there was in the utmost confusion by reason of some of the chief members, whom the Preachers had thought it needful to exclude from the society, and finding all I could write was not sufficient to stop the growing evil, I saw but one way remaining—to go myself and that as soon as possible. So the next day I took chaise with Mr. Goodwin and made straight for Mr. Bowen's at Llwyn-gwair in Pembrokeshire, hoping to borrow his sloop and so cross over to Dublin without delay.[4] I came to Llwyn-gwair on TUESDAY the 30th. The next

[1] The only reference in the Journal to Penmark, the family church of the Jones' of Fonmon, and even this may be a reference to the village rather than to the church. As far back as 1 Sept. 1745 Charles Wesley was virtually excluded from receiving Holy Communion there. Jackson, op. cit. i. 404.

[2] St. Martin's, a chapel-of-ease to Eglwysilan.

[3] 'Mr. Mathews'—the Thomas Mathews who married Diana Jones of Fonmon. He was sheriff of Glamorgan in 1769 and is said to have been 'a noted figure in Bath society' and to have fought a duel with Sheridan. He died in 1798 and was the last of the line of the Mathews of Llandaff. Williams, *Sheriffs of Glamorgan*, 67–8; *D.W.B.*, s.n. Mathew.

[4] There are no entries in the Journal between 31 Aug. (when Wesley preached at Gwennap in Cornwall) and 27 Sept. But it is clear from the *Letters* that he spent the greater part of September in Bristol, and that it was from there he set out on this visit to Ireland through South Wales. *Letters*, vi. 274–81.

day, OCTOBER 1st, the captain of a sloop at Fishguard, a small seaport town ten or twelve miles from Llwyn-gwair, sent me word he would sail for Dublin in the evening, but he did not stir till about eight the next evening. We had a small fair wind. From Fishguard to Dublin is about forty leagues. We had run ten or twelve till, at about eight in the morning, FRIDAY the 3rd, it fell dead calm. The swell was then such as I never felt before, except in the Bay of Biscay. Our little sloop, between twenty and thirty tons, rolled to and fro with a wonderful motion. About nine, the captain, finding he could not get forward, would have returned, but he could make no way. About eleven I desired we might go to prayer. Quickly after the wind sprung up fair, but it increased till, about eight at night, it blew a storm, and it was pitch dark so that having only the captain and a boy on board, we had much ado to work the vessel. However, about ten, though we scarce know how, we got safe into Dublin bay.[1]

XL

14–16 OCTOBER 1777

Dublin · Holyhead · Bangor · Tal-y-cafn(?) · Chester

MONDAY, 13 OCTOBER 1777. In the morning we went on board [at Dublin] but, the wind being right ahead and blowing hard, we made but little way till night, and the sea was so rough that I could not sleep till midnight.

TUESDAY, 14. After beating up and down several hours more the captain thought best to run under the Caernarvonshire shore. About noon we put out to sea again, but the storm increased and, about four, carried away our bowsprit and tore one of the sails to tatters. But the damage was soon repaired and before six, by the good providence of God, we landed at Holyhead.

---

[1] A few months later (on 5 Mar. 1778) Wesley, no doubt referring to this journey, informed Kitty Warren at Haverfordwest that he had hoped to leave Llwyn-gwair immediately, but 'we were providentially detained a little and a little and little longer, and I believe not in vain'. Telford, *Letters*, vi. 308.

Wanting to be in London as soon as possible, I took the chaise at seven and hastened to Bangor ferry. But here we were at a full stop. They could not, or would not, carry us over till one the next day, and they then gave us only two miserable horses, although I had paid beforehand (fool as I was) for four. At Conway ferry[1] we were stopped again so that, with all the speed we could possibly make, even with a chaise and four, we travelled eight and twenty miles yesterday and seventeen today! THURSDAY, in the afternoon, we reached Chester, Friday morning Lichfield, and on Saturday morning London.

XLI

12–29 AUGUST 1779

Gloucester · Monmouth · Brecon · Carmarthen · Llwyn-gwair
Newport · Haverfordwest · Trecwn · Little Newcastle
Haverfordwest · Pembroke · St. Daniel's · Haverfordwest
Carmarthen · Kidwelly · Llanelli · Swansea · Neath · Bridgend
Cowbridge · Llandaf · Cardiff · Newport · Bristol

WEDNESDAY, 11 AUGUST 1779. We went to Gloucester, where I preached with much satisfaction to a crowded audience.[2]

THURSDAY, 12. We went on to Monmouth where the late storm is blown over.[3] I preached at six in the evening but did not observe one inattentive person then any more than at five in the morning.

FRIDAY, 13. As I was going down a steep pair of stairs my foot slipped and I fell down several steps. Falling on the edge of one of

---

[1] i.e. at Conway or at Tal-y-cafn, some 7 miles from Llanrwst and 6 from Conway. Wesley describes the rough voyage from Dublin in more detail in a letter which he wrote from Bangor ferry on 15 Oct. to Mrs. Smyth, daughter of William Grattan, a wealthy Dublin goldsmith. Telford, *Letters*, vi. 282.

[2] Charles Wesley and his family accompanied him as far as Brecon.

[3] A little earlier (according to James Hall, one of Wesley's Preachers), the mob at Monmouth had given the Methodists much trouble. *Arm. Mag.*, 1793, 399.

them, it broke the case of an almanack which was in my pocket all
to pieces. The edge of another stair met my right buckle and snapped
the steel chape of it in two, but I was not hurt. So doth our good
Master give His angels charge over us! In the evening I preached
at Brecon and, leaving my brother there, on SATURDAY the
14th went forward to Carmarthen.

This evening, and in the morning, SUNDAY the 15th, the new
preaching-house[1] contained the congregation, but in the afternoon
we had, I think, the largest congregation I ever saw in Wales.
I preached on the Gospel for the day, the story of the Pharisee and
the Publican, and I believe many were constrained to cry out for
the present, 'God be merciful to me a sinner!'.

MONDAY, 16. In the evening I preached in the market-place
again to a very serious congregation, many of whom were in tears
and felt the word of God to be sharper than a two-edged sword.

TUESDAY, 17. Having some steep mountains to climb I took
a pair of post-horses. About four miles from the town one of them
began to kick and flounce without any visible cause, till he got one
of his legs over the pole. Br. Broadbent[2] and I then came out of the
chaise and walked forward. While the drivers were setting the chaise
right, the horses ran back almost to the town, so that we did not
reach Llwyn-gwair till between two and three o'clock. Mr. Bowen
was not returned from a journey to Glasgow. However, I spent
a very comfortable evening with Mrs. Bowen and the rest of the
family.

WEDNESDAY, 18. I preached about ten in Newport church and
then we went on to Haverfordwest. Here we had a very different
congregation both as to number and spirit, and we found the society
striving together for the hope of the gospel.

---

[1] Hardly the new (and second) building erected in 1771 by the Revd. Peter Williams
in Water Street (as suggested by M. H. Jones in *W.H.S. Proc.* ix. 89–90) but the first
Wesleyan Methodist chapel in Carmarthen. It stood in the yard of the Red Lion. *Vide
Bathafarn*, xxv. 40–1.

[2] John Broadbent, one of Wesley's Preachers, who was stationed on the Glamorgan
Circuit 1778–9 and who was about to leave it.

THURSDAY, 19. We went over to Trecwn, one of the loveliest places in Great Britain. The house stands in a deep valley, surrounded with tall woods and them with lofty mountains.[1] But as Admiral Vaughan was never married, this ancient family will soon come to an end. At two I preached in [Little] Newcastle church[2] and in the evening at Haverfordwest.

FRIDAY, 20. Many of us met at noon, and spent a solemn hour in intercession for our King and country.[3] In the evening, the house was thoroughly filled with people of all denominations. I believe that all felt that God was there, and that He was no respecter of persons.

SATURDAY, 21. I went to Pembroke. Understanding that a large number of American prisoners were here, in the evening I took my stand over against the place where they were confined, so that they all could hear distinctly. Many of them seemed much affected. Oh! that God may set their souls at liberty![4]

SUNDAY, 22. Mr. Rees,[5] a neighbouring clergyman, assisting me, I began at St. Daniel's between nine and ten. The congregation came from many miles round, and many of them were greatly refreshed. While we rode to Haverfordwest after dinner, I think it was full as hot as it used to be in Georgia, till about five o'clock a violent shower exceedingly cooled the air. But it ceased in half an hour, and we had then such a congregation as was scarce ever seen

[1] The house has now been demolished, but an ornamental stone under a tree near the former entrance to it still marks the spot where Wesley is alleged to have preached.

[2] *Vide* n. 5 below.

[3] Mr. L. J. Meyler of Milford Haven has suggested that the reason for this service of intercession was the appearance, five days earlier, of a French and Spanish fleet off Plymouth, and the capture of a number of British coasting vessels and a man-o'-war—an incident during the War of American Independence. *W.H.S. Proc.* xxi. 208.

[4] Wesley loyally supported the King and the government during this struggle once hostilities had broken out (despite his earlier sympathy with the colonists), and one of the tracts he wrote—his *Calm Address to the Inhabitants of England* (1777)—had a wide circulation and wielded considerable influence. Maldwyn Edwards, *John Wesley and the Eighteenth Century*, 70–81.

[5] The Revd. William Rees, incumbent of Little Newcastle from 1770 to 1782 (not, as Curnock seems to imply, the Revd. John Rees of Llangrannog); he was the only clergyman by the name of Rees in Pembrokeshire at this time. He was presented to the living by Sir Thomas Stepney, Bart. of Llanelli. *Church in Wales Records: SD/P/2647; West Wales Historical Records*, ii. 231.

here before. And though many of the gentry were there, yet a solemn awe spread over the whole assembly.

MONDAY, 23. I came once more to Carmarthen. Finding the people here (as indeed in every place) under a deep consternation through the terrible reports which flew on every side, I cried aloud in the market-place, 'Say ye unto the righteous, it shall be well with him'. God made it a word in season to them, and many where no longer afraid.

TUESDAY, 24. Setting out immediately after preaching, about eight I preached at Kidwelly, about nine miles from Carmarthen, to a very civil and unaffected congregation. At eleven, though the sun was intensely hot, I stood at the end of the churchyard in Llanelli and took occasion from a passing-bell strongly to enforce those words *It is appointed unto men once to die.* About six I preached at Swansea to a large congregation without feeling any weariness.

WEDNESDAY, 25. I preached at five and about eight in the Town Hall at Neath. In the afternoon I preached in the church[1] near Bridgend to a larger congregation than I ever saw there before; and at six in the Town Hall at Cowbridge, much crowded and hot enough. The heat made it a little more difficult to speak, but by the mercy of God I was no more tired when I had done than when I rose in the morning.

THURSDAY, 26. I preached at five and again at eleven. I think this was the happiest time of all. The poor and the rich seemed to be equally affected. Oh how are the times changed at Cowbridge since the people compassed the house where I was and poured in stones from every quarter! But my strength was then according to my day and (blessed by God) so it is still.

In the evening I preached in the large hall at Mr. Mathews' in Llandaf. And will the rich also hear the words of eternal life? *With God all things are possible.*

FRIDAY, 27. I preached at Cardiff about noon and at six in the evening. We then went on to Newport and, setting out early in the morning, reached Bristol in the afternoon.

[1] St. Mary's, Nolton.

XLII

14–15 APRIL 1781

Holyhead · Chester

MONDAY, 9 APRIL, 1781. Desiring to be in Ireland as soon as possible, I hastened to Liverpool and found a ship ready to sail; but the wind was contrary till, on Thursday, the captain came in haste and told us the wind was come quite fair. So Mr. Floyd, Snowden, Joseph Bradford and I, with two of our sisters, went on board; but scarce were we out at sea when the wind turned quite foul and rose higher and higher. In an hour I was so affected as I had not been for forty years before. For two days I could not swallow the quantity of a pea of anything solid, and very little of any liquid. I was bruised and sore from head to foot, and ill able to turn me on the bed. All Friday, the storm increasing, the sea, of consequence, was rougher and rougher. Early on SATURDAY morning [the 14th] the hatches were closed which, together with the violent motion, made our horses so turbulent that I was afraid we must have killed them lest they should damage the ship. Mrs. S. now crept to me, threw her arms over me and said, 'O sir, we will die together!' We had by this time three feet of water in the hold, though it was an exceeding light vessel. Meantime we were furiously driving on a lee shore, and when the captain cried, 'Helm a lee' she would not obey the helm. I called our brethren to prayers, and we found free access to the throne of grace. Soon after, we got, I know not how, into Holyhead harbour, after being sufficiently buffeted by the winds and waves for two days and two nights.

The more I considered, the more I was convinced it was not the will of God I should go to Ireland at this time. So we went into the stage-coach without delay and the next evening came to Chester.[1]

---

[1] Wesley then reconsidered his plans: should he go to the Isle of Man or 'those parts of Wales which I could not well see in my ordinary course'? After resting a day or two, he set out on 18 Apr. for Brecon via Whitchurch, Shrewsbury, and Worcester. In the event, he did not visit many new places in Wales; on the contrary, he followed his usual route to south-west Wales from Brecon.

XLIII

23 APRIL–15 MAY 1781

Worcester · Hay · Brecon · Carmarthen · Pembroke
Jeffreston · Pembroke · St. Daniel's · Haverfordwest
St. David's · Spital · Trecwn · Newport · Haverfordwest
Narberth · Carmarthen · Llanelli · Swansea · Neath
Bridgend · Cowbridge · Cardiff · Monmouth · Worcester

MONDAY, 23 APRIL 1781. Being informed it was fifty miles [from Worcester] to Brecon, we set out early but, on trial, we found they were computed miles. However, taking fresh horses at Hay, I just reached it in time, finding a large company waiting.

WEDNESDAY, 25. I set out for Carmarthen, but Joseph Bradford was so ill that after going six miles I left him at a friend's house and went only myself.[1] I came in good time to Carmarthen and enforced those solemn words on a serious congregation, *Now He commandeth all men everywhere to repent.*

THURSDAY, 26. I went on to Pembroke, and in the evening preached in the Town Hall.

FRIDAY, 27. I preached at Jeffreston, seven miles from Pembroke, to a large congregation of honest colliers. In the evening I preached in Pembroke Town Hall again to an elegant congregation and afterwards met the society, reduced to a fourth part of its ancient number. But as they are now all in peace and love with each other I trust they will increase again.

---

[1] Wesley left Joseph Bradford, one of his Preachers and travelling companion, at Beilie, a farm some 1½ miles from Defynnog; he remained there for three months. His hosts were Walter Williams and his wife, both of whom were members of the Brecon society. The husband died on 12 Mar. 1797 aged 54, his wife (formerly the widow of the Methodist John Watkins of Glanusk) on 12 Feb. 1825, aged 88. When Wesley called there on his last journey in 1790 at 6 a.m. (at 5, according to the Diary) he blessed one of their grandchildren who later became the Revd. W. R. M. Williams, M.A., a chaplain in the service of the East India Company. *Eurgrawn*, 1861, 372–5; 1862, 17–18.

SATURDAY, 28. We had in the evening the most solemn opportunity which I have had since we came into Wales, and the society seemed all alive and resolved to be *altogether Christians*.

SUNDAY, 29. At seven I preached in the room on *Lazarus, come forth* and about ten began at St. Daniel's.[1] The church was filled as usual and the Second Lesson gave me a suitable text, *Almost thou persuadest me to be a Christian*. I applied the words as closely as possible; and I doubt not some were more than *almost persuaded*. In the evening I preached at Haverfordwest to the liveliest congregation I have seen in Wales.

MONDAY, 30. I met about fifty children, such a company as I have not seen for many years. Miss Warren loves them and they love her. She has taken true pains with them and her labour has not been in vain. Several of them are much awakened and the behaviour of all is so composed that they are a pattern to the whole congregation.[2]

TUESDAY, 1 MAY. I rode to St. David's, seventeen measured miles from Haverfordwest. I was surprised to find all the land for the last nine or ten miles so fruitful and well cultivated. What a difference is there between the westernmost parts of England and the westernmost parts of Wales! The former (the west of Cornwall) so barren and wild, the latter so fruitful and well improved! But the town itself is a melancholy spectacle. I saw but one tolerable good house in it; the rest were miserable huts indeed. I do not remember so mean a town even in Ireland. The cathedral has been a large

[1] James Chubb, an English excise-man, rode to Pembroke from Narberth to hear Wesley on this occasion. He tells us that 'about 1500 attended the sacrament'. Later, he dined with him at 'Mr. Llewellin's' and accompanied him to the ferry. Wesley set out first on a pony, but though Chubb rode at 7 miles an hour, he failed to overtake him—and Wesley was then 77! *W.H.S. Proc.* xxix. 34.

[2] On an unspecified earlier visit (but before 1779), Wesley had committed to the care of Miss Catherine Warren (a sister of the Lady Kensington of the day) a number of children, apparently all boys, whom she taught. By 1784 Catherine (or Kitty, as Wesley called her) had 'grown weary of well-doing and had totally given up her charge'. But she had resumed it once again by the following year. *W.H.S. Proc.* xxx. 132–3; Telford, *Letters*, vii. 229. She frequently corresponded with Wesley and evidently discussed circuit matters with him. E.g. Telford, *Letters*, vi. 308, 319, 328–9, 334, 359.

and stately fabric, far superior to any other in Wales, but a great part of it is fallen down already and the rest is hastening into ruin— one blessed fruit (among many) of bishops residing at a distance from their see. Here are the tombs and effigies of many ancient worthies, Owen Tudor[1] in particular. But the zealous Cromwellians broke off their noses, hands and feet and defaced them as much as possible. But what had the Tudors done to them? Why, they were progenitors of kings.

THURSDAY, 3. About ten I preached at Spital, a large village about six miles from Haverfordwest. Thence we went to Trecwn and spent a few hours in that lovely retirement, buried from all the world in the depth of woods and mountains.

FRIDAY, 4. About eleven I preached in Newport church and again at four in the evening. SATURDAY the 5th I returned to Haverfordwest.

SUNDAY, 6. I preached in St. Thomas' church on *We preach Christ crucified*.[2] It was a stumbling to some of the hearers. So the Scripture is fulfilled. But I had amends when I met the society in the evening.

MONDAY, 7. About ten I preached near the market-place in Narberth, a large town ten miles east from Haverfordwest.[3] Abundance of people flocked together and they were all as still as night. In the evening I preached to an equally attentive congregation at Carmarthen.

[1] Not Owen Tudor's tomb but that of his son Edmund, whose son became Henry VII, the first of the Tudor dynasty of England.
[2] The rector of St. Thomas, Haverfordwest, from 1777 to 1799 was the Revd. William Cleaveland. *West Wales Historical Records*, ii. 197.
[3] James Chubb was the means of introducing Methodism into Narberth. He lived there for twelve months (some time between 1780 and 1784, and probably in 1780–1) and arranged for Wesley's Preachers to visit the place once a fortnight and preach in a room which he had found for them. He was also on good terms with the Calvinistic Methodists; he attended some of their meetings, and they attended some of the Wesleyan services. *W.H.S. Proc.* xxix. 28.

TUESDAY, 8. I had a large congregation at Llanelli and at Swansea. Some months since, there were abundance of hearers at Neath, but on a sudden one lying tongue set the society on fire till almost half of them were scattered away. But as all, offended or not offended, were at the Town Hall, I took the opportunity of strongly enforcing the Apostle's words, *Let all bitterness and wrath and anger and clamour and evil-speaking be put away from you, with all malice.* I believe God sealed His word on many hearts and we shall have better days at Neath. About three, I preached in the church near Bridgend, and at six in the Town Hall at Cowbridge.

THURSDAY, 10. I preached in our room[1] about ten on *I am not ashamed of the gospel of Christ.* May God deliver us from this evil disease which eats out all the heart of religion! In the evening I preached in the Town Hall at Cardiff, but the congregation was almost wholly new. The far greater part of the old society, Ann Jenkins, Thomas Glascott, Arthur Price, Jane Haswell, Nancy Newell and a long train are gone hence and are no more seen. And how few are followers of them as they were of Christ!

MONDAY, 14. Before I reached Monmouth one met and informed me that Mr. C.,[2] a Justice of the Peace, one of the greatest men in the town, desired I would take a bed at his house. Of consequence, all the rabble of the town were as quiet as lambs and we had a comfortable opportunity both night and morning. Surely this is the Lord's doing!

TUESDAY, 15. We went through miserable roads to Worcester.

---

[1] The Methodists of Cowbridge had erected a meeting-house between the Conference of Aug. 1780 and Wesley's visit. *Min. of Conf.* i. 146; *J.H.S.P.C.W.* xl. 42. The leader of the society was Isaac Skinner.

[2] Probably the same person as the Mr. G. referred to on 15 Aug. 1788. If so, William Catchmay(d), who assumed the name of Gwinnett by licence on 17 Aug. 1782 on inheriting Shurdington, near Chippenham, from Mary, widow of George Gwinnett. Bradney, *History of Monmouth*, Part 1, vol. ii, 215–17.

XLIV

DECEMBER 1781

Wrexham

On 6 January 1782 Miss Hester Ann Roe told John Wesley:[1]

I was surprised to hear that you had been at Chester and Wrexham

to which Wesley replied on 17 January from London:[2]

I have never at all repented of my late journey to Chester; a flame was kindled both there and at Wrexham which, I trust, will not soon be put out.

That is quite explicit: John Wesley visited Wrexham, though there is no reference to the visit in his Journal. It is clear, too, that on this same journey he visited Chester. The only doubt surrounds the date. Telford, the editor of the Standard Edition of Wesley's Letters, assumed that in the above letter Wesley was referring to the visit which he made to Chester in April 1781, when the storm recorded in Journey XLII had prevented his sailing from Liverpool to Ireland.[3]

But Wesley wrote a letter *from Chester* on 15 December 1781 to Miss Ann Loxdale, Dr. Thomas Coke's second wife, who was then living at Shrewsbury. Telford printed the letter in his Standard Edition, but under the date 15 April, not 15 December.[4] In this instance he merely followed F. F. Bretherton, the author of *Early Methodism in and around Chester*, and probably assumed, as Bretherton had assumed before him, that as the Journal contains no reference to a visit to Chester in 1781 other than the one made in April (and has no entries of any kind between 12 and 28 December), '15 December' was a slip of the pen for '15 April'. Later, and after the *Letters* had appeared, Bretherton queried the assumption he had made, without, however, being able to clarify the matter to his satisfaction.[5]

It was a large assumption to make. In the first place, would John Wesley, writing on 17 January 1782, refer to a journey he had

[1] *Arm. Mag.*, 1790, 108.   [2] Telford, *Letters*, vii. 100.   [3] Ibid., n. 1.
[4] Ibid., 59.   [5] *W.H.S. Proc.* xviii. 76–7.

made nine months earlier as 'my late journey'? On the face of it, it seems hardly likely; 'my last journey' or 'the journey I made last year to Chester' would have been more apposite. Moreover, he could have expressed his satisfaction with that visit in another letter which he had written to Miss Roe on 9 December 1781—a mere six weeks earlier.[1] On the other hand, if in fact he had visited Chester and Wrexham after 9 December it would have been perfectly natural for Miss Roe to express her surprise on 6 January and for Wesley to have termed it his 'late journey'. Again, though Wesley was no more infallible than other mortals, to insert '15 December' on his letter when in fact he meant '15 April' (and writing, as he must have been on this assumption, in spring not in mid-winter) would have been an unusually strange lapse. And finally, the negative argument which first Bretherton and then Telford deduced from the silence of the Journal simply will not do. For we know from other sources that Wesley visited dozens of places without mentioning them in his Journal; Wrexham indeed is a case in point. There is no more reason for asserting that he did not visit Chester in 1781 after 15 April merely because he omitted to mention it in his Journal than there is for assuming that he did not visit Wrexham for the same reason. But whereas Bretherton and Telford rejected the one, they accepted the other.

In short, the evidence, such as it is, in favour of Wesley's having made another visit to Chester in 1781 but later than 15 April is stronger than the negative deduction from silence; when Wesley wrote his letter from Chester on 15 December 1781 he was probably in the city on that date. But when did he visit Wrexham? He could have called there during his stay at Chester, on his way thither, or on his way back to London. He was at Chatham on 12 December and in London on the 28th. Previous journeys from Chester to London had taken him two days. Allowing him therefore two days to reach the city and two days to return to the capital, it seems reasonable to infer that he visited Wrexham between 14 and 26 December 1781—and, in view of Christmas falling within this period, probably nearer the 14th than the 26th.

It only remains to add that a strong local tradition exists that

[1] Telford, op. cit., vii. 95–6.

Wesley visited Wrexham; that he preached from an upper window of a house on Town Hill occupied by one Benjamin Parry; that some years later another member of the family, Molly Parry, retained the armchair in which Wesley sat while taking tea; and that later still this chair was presented to the trustees of Brynffynnon Methodist church in the town. *Vide Bathafarn*, xviii. 22–41.

XLV
10–11 APRIL 1783

*Chester · Holywell · St. Asaph · Conway · Bangor · Gwindy
Holyhead · Dunleary*

[John Wesley was at Nottingham on 4 April 1783 and thence set out for Ireland via Chester and North Wales. He dismissed this journey in a single sentence in his Journal.]

THURSDAY, 10 APRIL

4, Prayed [—]; 5, chaise, Holywell; 12, St. Asaph, dinner, chaise, Conway, writ narrative, prayed; 8, supper, conversed; 9.45.

FRIDAY, 11

4 Prayed; 5, chaise; 8, Bangor Ferry, tea, chaise; 11.30, Gwindy,[1] dinner, chaise; 3, Holyhead, tea, writ narrative; 5.30, on the 'Bestboran'; 8, lay down.

SATURDAY, 12

4, Sleep, in talk, walk; 8, tea, prayed, dozed, prayed, tea; 9 sleep.

SUNDAY, 13

4.30, Drest, conversed; 6, in the boat; 7, Dunleary. . . .

TUESDAY, 1 APRIL 1783

I went through several of the societies till I reached Holyhead on FRIDAY the 11th. We went on board without delay and on

[1] An inn, built *c.* 1758, on the old post road across Anglesey, between Bodedern and Bodffordd, in the parish of Llandrygarn. D. W. Wiliam in *Trans. Anglesey Ant. Soc.*, 1967, 28–40.

SUNDAY morning landed at Dunleary, whence (not being able to procure a carriage) I walked on to Dublin.

XLVI

8–9 MAY 1783

Dublin · Holyhead · Chester

THURSDAY, 8 MAY 1783

1, Tea, prayer, coach; 2.30, in the boat; 4, on board; 5, sailed, Captain Cook; 6.30, tea, Cook; 12, dinner, Cook; 5.30, Holyhead on business; 7, coach; 9, Gwindy, supper; 10.30.

FRIDAY, 9

3.30, On business; 4, coach, prayed, Sur[vey] of Ireland*; 10 Conway, tea, boat; 11, coach,* Survey, within; *9, Chester, at Miss Beddish, supper, conversed, prayer; 10.45.*

THURSDAY, 8 MAY 1783

We rose at one [in Dublin], went down to the quay at two, and about four went on board the *Hillsborough* packet. About five the wind turned fair and between five and six in the evening brought us to Holyhead. About seven we took coach, and the next evening met our friends at Chester.

XLVII

9–28 AUGUST 1784

Ledbury · Ross · Monmouth · Brecon · Carmarthen · Tenby Pembroke · St. Daniel's · Haverfordwest · Roch · Trecwn Llwyn-gwair · Newport · Haverfordwest · Carmarthen · Cardiff Newport · Bristol

MONDAY, 9 AUGUST, 1784

4, Prayed, Psa. lxii, 1, select society [at Worcester], in talk, tea; 7, chaise; 10, Ledbury, tea, visited; 11, chaise; 1.30, Ross, dinner;

2.30, chaise; 4.30, Monmou[th], tea, conversed, prayed; 6, Jo. xvii, 3! Mag.,[1] supper, together, prayer; 9.30.

I rode over Malvern Hills, which afford one of the finest prospects in the kingdom, to Ledbury then through miserable roads to Ross. I preached in the evening at Monmouth to a very quiet and civil congregation. Tumults were now at an end, as I lodged at the house of a gentleman whom none cared to oppose.[2] And even in the morning we had a large congregation, both of rich and poor.

TUESDAY, 10

4, Prayed, 1 Pet. ii, 1, etc., Mag.; 8, tea, conversed, Journal; 12, walk; 1.15, dinner, within; 2.30, prayed; 3, Lu. vii, 36! at brother John's, tea, conversed, prayer; 6, 1 Cor. xiii, 1! walk together; 8, supper, conversed, prayer; 9.45.

I took a walk to what is called the Bowling-green House, not a mile from the town. I have hardly seen such a place before. A gravel walk leads through the most beautiful meadows, surrounded on all sides by fruitful hills, to a gently rising ground on the top of which is a smooth green on which the gentry of the town frequently spend the evening in dancing. From hence spread various walks bordered with flowers, one of which leads down to the river, on the back of which runs another walk whose artless shades are not penetrated by the sun. These are full as beautiful in their kind as even the hanging woods at Brecon.[3]

WEDNESDAY, 11

4, Prayed, writ narrative; 6, Heb. vi, 1, tea, conversed, prayer; 8, chaise; 11, Ab[er]gav[enny]; 11, tea; 12, chaise; 3.30, Brecon, at brother Church,[4] on business, dinner, letters; 5.30, prayed; 6.30, Isai. lix, 1, 2! society, writ narrative, supper, prayer; 9.30.

[1] i.e. the *Arminian Magazine*, which Wesley edited and which first appeared in 1778.

[2] The 'brother John's' of the Diary, i.e. the Mr. Johnson with whom he lodged again on 15 Aug. 1788.

[3] The description fits Beaulieu Grove on the Kymin, though the Summer House (now the Round House) was not erected until 1794 and the Naval Temple until 1800 (C. Heath, *A Descriptive Account of the Kymin Summer House . . .* 2nd edition, 1800; *Bathafarn*, xxv. 39-40.) It probably reminded Wesley of the Priory Groves, Brecon.

[4] John Church, Ffrwd-grech, the society steward (not William Churchey as in Curnock, vii. 9).

It was with some difficulty that I broke from this affectionate people and went on through a most lovely country to Brecon.

THURSDAY, 12

4, Prayed, Rom. xiii, 11 etc, letters; 8, tea, conversed, Accounts, letters; 12, walk; 1.30, dinner, conversed; 2.30, letters; 4.30, prayed, tea, conversed; 6.30, Prov. iii, 17! visited!; 8, supper, within, prayer; 9.30.

I found the little flock were in great peace and increasing in number as well as in strength. I preached in the Town Hall. I never saw such a congregation in Brecon before, no, not even when I preached abroad. And I scarce ever found the power of God so present. It seemed as if everyone must know the Lord, from the least to the greatest.

FRIDAY, 13

3.30, on business; 4, chaise, Penpont,¹ tea, prayer, chaise; 9.15 Llando[very], tea; 10, chaise; 12, Llandeilo; 1, dinner, conversed; 2, chaise; 4.30, Carma[rthen], at sister Lewis's,² tea, conversed, prayed; 6, Isa. lxvi; 8, supper, prayer; 9.30.

We went on to Carmarthen. After preaching, I advised all the audience to copy after the decent behaviour of the Hollanders in and after public worship. They all took my advice; none opened their lips till they came into the open air.³

SATURDAY, 14

4, Prayed, Phil. ii, 12!, tea; 6.30, chaise; 10, Tavernspite,⁴ tea; 10.45, chaise; 1.15, Tenb[y], at Captain Fa[rr's], Mag., dinner;

---

¹ Possibly at the home of Robert Phillips, a smith and John Prickard's friend, who formerly lived at Brecon. T. Wynne Jones, *Wes. Meth. in Brecon Circuits*, 99; *Eurgrawn*, 1862, 17–18.

² Susannah(?) Lewis, a member of the Carmarthen society. *Meth. Mag.*, 1805, 506–7.

³ Wesley had been impressed by the decorous behaviour of the Dutch during and at the close of church services in June 1783.

⁴ A reminder that Wesley sometimes visited and preached at places not mentioned in his Journal.

3, Mag.; prayed, walk!; 5, tea, conversed; 6, 2 Cor. viii, 9, con-
versed, supper, prayer, on business; 9.45.

Was the hottest day we have had this summer. We reached Tenby
soon after one. After dinner we took a walk through the town.
I think there is not such a town in England. It is the Kilmallock
of Great Britain. Two-thirds of the ancient town are either in ruins
or vanished away.[1] In the evening I preached in the street to a large
congregation of rich and poor, all quiet and attentive. I cannot but
think salvation is at length come to this town also.

SUNDAY, 15

4, Prayed, Mag.; 6, Rom. xii, 1; 7.30, chaise; 9.30, Pembroke,
tea, conversed, read; 10.30, St. Dan[iel's], read prayers, Acts
xiii, 26!, communion; 1, hymns; 2, dinner, conversed, hymns,
prayed, tea; 6, Lu. xix, 42!; supper, prayer; 9.45.

I preached again in the morning, SUNDAY the 15th, and the
word seemed to sink into the hearts of the hearers. Thence we went
by Pembroke to St. Daniel's. It was a comfortable season. We had
such another at Pembroke in the evening. Many mourned after
God and many rejoiced with joy unspeakable.

MONDAY, 16

4, Prayed, letters; 7.15, tea, conversed, prayer; 8, Matt. xii, 41,
letter; 9.30, read, chaise; 12.30, Hav[erford]west, at Mr. Davis,
hymns; 2, dinner, conversed; 3.30, letters, prayed; 5.30, tea,
conversed; 6.30, Matt. vii, 24!, society, supper, conversed, prayer;
9.15.

I preached at Haverfordwest.

TUESDAY, 17

4, Prayed, 1 Cor. xii, 31! letters, texts; 8, tea, conversed, prayer;
9.15, rode; 11, Roach, Eph. iv, 1 etc, rode; 1.15, at sister Warren's;

---

[1] On 29 May 1749 Wesley described Kilmallock (some 21 miles south of Limerick)
as 'once a large and strong city, now a heap of ruins'. Curnock, op. cit., iii. 402.

2, visited, dinner, conversed, prayer; 3.30, on business, prayed, tea, conversed; 6.30, Rom. viii, 4, society, supper, prayer; 9.30.

We rode over to Roch, eight miles from Haverfordwest. The new preaching-house was pretty-well filled,[1] and I was glad to find that a little ride did me no harm.

WEDNESDAY, 18

4, Prayed, Jud. i, 27; walk, letter; 8, tea, conversed, prayer, visited; 10.15, chaise; 12.45, Trecwn, within; 2, dinner, together; 3.15, writ narrative; 5, tea, conversed, prayed, writ narrative; 7, Phil. iii, 8, supper, within, prayer; 9.45.

I went to Admiral Vaughan's at Trecwn, one of the pleasantest seats in Great Britain. The house is embosomed in lofty woods and does not appear till you drop down upon it. The Admiral governs his family, as he did his ship, with the utmost punctuality. The bell rings and all attend without delay, whether at meals or at morning and evening prayer. I preached at seven on *Phil.* iii, 8 and spent the evening in serious conversation.

THURSDAY, 19

4, Prayed, letters; 8, prayer, tea, conversed; 9.15, chaise, visited; 12.30 Ll[wy]n-gwair; 1, together; 2.30, dinner, conversed; 4, prayed, tea, Matt. vii, 16!, supper, together, prayer, hymns.

I went on to Mr. Bowen's at Llwyn-gwair, another agreeable place, the more so because of the company—Mr. and Mrs. Bowen, his brother, and six of their eleven children, two of whom are lately come from the University.[2]

FRIDAY, 20

4, Prayed, letter; 7, Rom. viii, 3, 4, tea, conversed, chaise, Newport, prayers; 9, 1 Sam. xxi, 8!; 9.30, chaise; 11.15, New[castle],

---

[1] Prior to the opening of the preaching-house in 1784, the Roch society met for many years in the house of Henry Child. *Wes. Meth. Mag.*, 1836, 139–40.

[2] George and Easter (or Hester) Bowen had twelve children, six sons and six daughters, but one of the sons had died in infancy. For the Bowen family, *vide* W. Islwyn Morgan in *Bathafarn*, xxii. 37–48; xxiii. 14–24.

*Jo. ii, 12!, chaise, Hav[erfordwest], within, dinner, visited many,
tea, prayer; 6.30, Jo. iv, 24, supper, prayer; 10.*

About eight I preached in the church at Newport and spoke strong
words, if haply some might awake out of sleep. Thence we went to
Haverfordwest, it being the day when the bishop held his visitation.
As I was returning in the afternoon from visiting some of the poor
people, a carriage in the street obliged me to walk very near a clergyman who made me a low bow. I did the same to him, though I did
not then know the bishop, who has indeed won the hearts of the
people in general by his courteous and obliging behaviour.[1]

SATURDAY, 21

*4, Prayed, Rev. xiv, 1 etc, tea, prayer; 6.30, chaise, Narbe[rth],
Heb. ix, 27; 9.30, chaise; 1.45, Carma[rthe]n; 2.15, dinner,
letters, prayed; 5, tea, conversed, letters; 7, Matt. xi, 30!, supper,
together, prayer, on business; 9.30.*

SUNDAY, 22

*4, Prayed, letters, tea; 8, Col. iii, 11, letters; 11, prayers!; 1,
dinner, conversed; 2, writ narrative; 3, prayed, tea, conversed; 5,
Lu. xviii, 10, society, visited, supper, conversed, prayer; 9.30.*

I heard a good sermon in the church at Carmarthen (being the
Assize sermon) on *There is no power but of God.* In the evening I
preached in the market-place to, I think, the largest congregation
I ever saw in Wales.

MONDAY, 23

*4, Prayed, Heb. ii, 3!; letter, tea; 7.30, chaise; 11, Llanell[i],
Heb. xii, 14; 12.30, dinner; 1.45, chaise [cipher ⌐]; 4.30, Swansea, tea, conversed, on business; 6, Psa. xxiv, 3, 4!, writ narrative,
supper, conversed, prayer; 9.45.*

TUESDAY, 24

*4, Prayed, tea; 4.45, chaise, Nea[th], tea, conversed; 8, Psa. cxliv,
15!, chaise; 4, Cow[bridge], at Mr. Thomas's, on business, tea,*

---

[1] The bishop of St. David's, 1783–8, was Edward Smallwell.

converded, writ narrative; 6.30, Mic. ii, 10, society, within, supper; prayer; 9.45.

WEDNESDAY, 25

4, Prayed, Mag.; 8, tea, conversed, prayer, letters, Mag.; 11, prayers, Rev. xx, 12; 1, chaise; 2.30, Fonmon,¹ Mag.; 3, dinner, together; 4, Mag., prayed, tea; 6, Job. xxii, 21!, Mag., supper, conversed, prayers; 10, ill.

THURSDAY, 26

5.15, Prayed; 6, Mag.; 8, Lu. xii, 7!, tea, conversed, Mag., prayer; 11, chaise; 1.30, Llandaf, read Volta[ire]; 2.30, dinner, within; 4, Volta[ire], chaise; 5, Cardiff, tea, read, prayed; 6, Acts xi, 26, society, supper, conversed, prayer; 9.30.

On the road I read over Voltaire's Memoirs of himself. Certainly never was a more consummate coxcomb! But even his character is less horrid than that of his royal hero! Surely so unnatural a brute never disgraced a throne before! *Cedite, Romani Catamiti! Cedite, Graii!* A monster that made it a fixed rule to let no woman and no priest enter his palace, that not only glorified in the constant policy of sodomy himself but made it free for all his subjects! What a pity that his father had not beheaded him in his youth and saved him from all this sin and shame!²

In the evening I preached in the Town Hall at Cardiff and shewed the scriptural meaning of that much-mistaken word, a Christian.

FRIDAY, 27

4, Prayed, Mag.; 8, tea, letter; 9, Matt. xxii, 4; 10.15, chaise; 12.15, Parsley Works, walk; 2, dinner, conversed, prayer, chaise;

---

¹ This visit to Fonmon doubtless explains the letter written two days later by Wesley to Robert Jones, jun. in which he advised him to go to Utrecht rather than France, if he decided to go abroad—as he did, to escape from his creditors. *Wesley Letters:* 22, printed in Telford, *Letters*, vii. 232.

² Frederick the Great.

4, Newport, prayed, Mag., tea; 6, Luke xiii, 23!, Mag., supper, prayer; 9.30.

I preached at Newport. I hardly know such another place. The people hear and hear and are as much moved as the benches they sit upon. I spoke as strong as I possibly could on *Awake thou that sleepest*, and I judged from the number who attended at five in the morning that it was not all lost labour.

SATURDAY, 28

4, Prayed, Eph. vi, 14!, tea; 6.30, chaise; 9.15, Passage, tea, Mag.; 1, dinner, Mag., prayed; 6, boat; 6.30 Inn; 7, chaise; 8.30, at sister Jo[hn]son['s]; 9, supper, prayer, on business; 10, ill.

Being informed the boat would pass at eight, we hastened to the New Passage. But we were time enough, for it did not set out till past six in the evening. However, we got into the boat about[1] seven and before nine reached Bristol.

XLVIII

8–10 APRIL 1785

Chester · Holyhead · Dublin

WEDNESDAY, 6 APRIL 1785. I preached at Liverpool, but I found no ship there ready to sail. So THURSDAY the 7th (after preaching at Warrington in the way) I hastened to Chester. Neither was there any ship at Parkgate ready to sail, so FRIDAY the 8th we took coach and reached Holyhead between four and five on SATURDAY in the afternoon. Between nine and ten we went on board the *Clermont* packet. But it was dead calm till past ten on SUNDAY the 10th, when the company desired me to give them a sermon. After sermon I prayed that God would give us a full and speedy passage. While I was speaking the wind sprung

---

[1] Samuel Bradburn corrected this in his copy of the Journal to 'got out of the boat'. *W.H.S. Proc.* xix. 115.

up and in twelve hours brought us to Dublin bay. Does not our Lord still hear the prayer?

XLIX

11–13 JULY 1785

Dublin · Holyhead · Gwindy · Kinmel · Chester

SUNDAY, 10 JULY 1785. I went on board the *Prince of Wales*, one of the neatest ships I ever was in. We left the work of God increasing in every part of the kingdom,[1] more than it has done for many years. About two in the morning we sailed out of Dublin bay and came to Holyhead before one in the afternoon on MONDAY, the 11th. That evening we went on to Gwindy, TUESDAY the 12th to Kinmel, one of the pleasantest inns[2] in Wales, surrounded with gardens and stately woods which the late proprietor must see no more!

WEDNESDAY, 13. We reached Chester.

L

5 APRIL 1787

Chester · Conway · Holyhead · Dublin

WEDNESDAY, 4 APRIL 1787. I went to Chester and preached in the evening on *Heb.* iii, 12. Finding there was no packet at Parkgate I immediately took places in the mail-coach for Holyhead.[3]

---

[1] i.e. Ireland. On 26 June he had written from Dublin to inform Miss Elizabeth Ritchie of Otley of this progress. Tyerman, *Wesley*, iii. 461.

[2] The Cross Foxes, Kinmel. *Bathafarn*, ii. 47.

[3] About 1776 the landlord of the White Lion inn, Chester, began to carry passengers daily (except Sundays) by 'flying post-chaise' to Holyhead for two guineas. A regular coach service soon followed. Some three years later Robert Lawrence of the Raven and Bell inn, Shrewsbury, started a rival service along the same route, via Wrexham and Mold. The first G.P.O. mail-coach from Chester to Holyhead did not run until 1785; it replaced the former post-boys on horseback. A. H. Dodd, *Arch. Camb.*, 1925, 143.

The porter called us at two in the morning on THURSDAY, but came again in half an hour to inform us the coach was full, so they returned my money and at four I took a post-chaise. We overtook the coach at Conway and, crossing the ferry with the passengers, went forward without delay. So we came to Holyhead an hour before them and went on board the *Le Despencer* between eleven and twelve o'clock. At one we left the harbour and at two the next day came into Dublin bay.

LI

15–30 AUGUST 1788

*Gloucester · Monmouth · Brecon · Carmarthen · Llwyn-gwair
Newport · Llwyn-gwair · Trecwn · Haverfordwest · Pembroke
St. Daniel's · Haverfordwest · Carmarthen · Kidwelly
Llanelli · Swansea · Neath · Ffontygari · Cowbridge
Ffontygari · Cardiff · Bristol*

FRIDAY, 15 AUGUST 1788.[1] We went on [from Gloucester] to Monmouth, but Mr. G.[2] has done with us, so I lodged with my old friend Mr. Johnson,[3] and instead of that lovely young woman S.B.,[4] who is removed to Cowbridge, met with her youngest sister, who more than supplies her place. She is a jewel indeed, full of

[1] Wesley had evidently been delayed, for he told Kitty Warren on 22 July that he hoped to be in Monmouth on 8 Aug. and at Cowbridge on the 20th. He was accompanied for part of the journey by William Stevens, newly appointed Preacher to the Glamorgan Circuit. Telford, *Letters*, viii. 75; *Meth. Mag.*, 1814, 568.

[2] Not a misprint for 'Mr. C.' (as in Curnock, vii. 425 n. 1) but Mr. W. C. Gwinnett (*ante*, p. 107 n. 2). On 27 Oct. 1784 Wesley told Sarah Baker: 'Ap erson of Mr. Gwinnett's rank and influence is quite an overmatch for twenty petty rioters.' Telford, *Letters*, vii. 245. *Vide* also C. Heath, *Historical and Descriptive Accounts of . . . the Town of Monmouth, passim.*

[3] Thomas Johnson? If so, he was four times mayor of Monmouth between 1776 and 1808. He died 12 Nov. 1815, aged 84. Bradney, op. cit., vol. 1, Part 1, 2, and memorial tomb in St. Mary's churchyard.

[4] Sarah Baker who, according to Wesley, had done 'unspeakable good' since she came to Cowbridge. Telford, *Letters*, viii. 88–9. Her sister Elizabeth married a Mr. Jordan of Monmouth and died at Maryland in the Monmouth Circuit on 23 Dec. 1843, aged 85. *Wes. Meth. Mag.*, 1844, 244.

faith and love, and zealous of good works. I preached both in the evening and the next morning with the demonstration of the Spirit, and all the congregation, rich and poor, appeared to be sensible of it.

SATURDAY, 16. We had an easy journey to Brecon, where I preached in the evening.

SUNDAY, 17. I preached in the room at eight on the fruit of the Spirit. In the evening, I preached in the spacious Town Hall, so filled as it had never been before. I think there is a little company here that are truly alive to God.

MONDAY, 18. I went on to Carmarthen and preached at six on 2 *Cor.* v, 19 and again at five in the morning, TUESDAY the 19th, when the room was well filled. A servant of Mr. Bowen's came early in the morning to show us the way to Llwyn-gwair, and it was well he did for I do not know that we could otherwise have found our way thither. We met (as I expected) with a hearty welcome. At five I preached in Newport church to a large congregation and with a greater prospect of doing good than ever I had before. We passed an agreeable evening at Llwyn-gwair.

WEDNESDAY, 20. I went to Trecwn, one of the most venerable seats in Great Britain. The good old house is buried in woods and mountains, having no resemblance to any place I have seen. It is just suited to the good old Admiral with his four maiden sisters, the youngest of whom, I suppose, has lived more than seventy years. I preached at twelve, and in the afternoon went on to Haverford-west. The room was filled sufficiently and I could not but believe God will build up the waste places.

THURSDAY, 21. The room was well filled at five. Finding there had been no discipline here for some time, I determined to begin at the foundation and settle everything. So I first visited and regulated the classes, then restored the bands, which had been totally neglec-ted, and then gave directions for meeting the leaders both of bands and classes. After preaching in the evening I met the society and gave them a warm exhortation to set out anew. I trust they will; and all the present preachers, I am persuaded, will neglect nothing.[1]

FRIDAY, 22. I went to Pembroke. Here likewise not one thing but everything had been neglected. No stewards, no bands, half of the preaching-places dropped, all the people cold, heartless, dead! I spoke earnestly in the evening and the word was as fire. Surely some fruit will follow!

SUNDAY, 24. We had a lovely congregation at St. Daniel's and a remarkable blessing. In the afternoon I returned to Haverfordwest and preached in a large open space near the great church, to such a congregation as I have not seen in Wales for many years. I explained and applied the parable of the Sower, and God clothed his word with power. I know not whether I have had such an opportunity before since I left London.

MONDAY, 25. I spent another night at Carmarthen very agreeably.

TUESDAY, 26. I preached in Kidwelly at nine, between twelve and one at Llanelli (to all the gentry in the town!) and in the evening to a multitude of people at Swansea.

WEDNESDAY, 27. Far more than the room would contain attended at five in the morning. About eight I preached in our new preaching-house at Neath,[2] and in the afternoon reached Ffontygari and found Mrs. Jones, with several of her children about her, on the margin of the grave, worn out with that dread disease—a cancer. She uttered no complaint but was all patience and resignation, showing the dignity of a Christian in weakness and pain and death.[3]

---

[1] William Palmer, C. Bond, and Francis Truscott had just been appointed to the Pembrokeshire Circuit in the place of William Dufton, Simon Day, and S. Kessall.

[2] The Conference of 1787 had approved the proposal to build a preaching-house in Neath. *Min. of Conf.*, i. 203.

[3] Mrs. Robert Jones, of Fonmon and Ffontygari, died on 19 Sept. 1788—'a very sober and religious gentlewoman', wrote the Diarist William Thomas. In her will, she left John Wesley 'or the chief of his Society' the sum of ten guineas for the term of ten years after her death. *Bathafarn*, ix. 43.

I preached on *It is appointed unto men once to die*, and I believe all present felt the awful truth.

I had intended to go on to Cowbridge the next day, but being much importuned to give one day more to a dying friend, I yielded and desired another preacher to go and supply my place. In the evening I preached on *Ps.* cxlvi, 3, 4. The scene before us greatly confirmed the word.

FRIDAY, 29. That they might not be offended, I went to Cow-bridge. In half an hour's notice we had a large congregation in the Town Hall, to whom I showed the nature and pleasantness of religion from *Prov.* iii, 17. I returned to Ffontygari, took my leave of the dying saint, and then went on to Cardiff. In the evening I preached (probably for the last time) to a very genteel congregation in the Town Hall.

SATURDAY, 30. I returned to Bristol.

LII

26–7 MARCH 1789

Shrewsbury · Oswestry · Llanrwst · Conway · Bangor
Gwindy · Holyhead · Dublin

THURSDAY, 26 MARCH, 1789

3.30, Tea; 4.30, chaise; 8, Oswestry, tea; 9, chaise [——]; 12, chaise; 1.30, dinner; 2.30, chaise; 5.30, horses; 8, Llanrwst, supper, on business; 10.

We set out early [from Shrewsbury] and taking post-horses at Llanrwst reached Conway between eight and nine o'clock, having travelled 78 miles that day, 28 more than from Chester to Conway.[1]

[1] There is obviously a discrepancy between the Diary and the Journal for this visit. According to the Diary, Wesley arrived at Conway from Llanrwst about 8 a.m. on the 27th after staying overnight at Llanrwst, but according to the Journal he got there between 8 and 9 p.m. on the 26th. F. F. Bretherton suggested (*W.H.S. Proc.* xix. 151) reading 'to Llanrwst' for 'at Llanrwst' and adding 'next morning' after 'Conway'. This would certainly accord with the Diary.

FRIDAY, 27

4.30, chaise; 8, Conway, tea; 9, chaise, read Watson; 11.30,
Bangor Ferry, chaise; 3.15, Gwindy; 4.30, chaise; 6, Holyhead,
tea, within; on board the Clermont; *12, sailed, cramp!*

We went on to Holyhead, and at eight in the evening went on board
the *Clermont*[1] packet. The wind stood fair three or four hours. It
then turned against us and blew hard. I do not remember I was ever
so sick at sea before, but this was little to the cramp which held most
of the night with little intermission.

SATURDAY, 28

6, Not walk [——]!, together, prayer; 10 [——]; 9 lay down.

All SATURDAY we were beating to and fro and gaining little
ground, and I was so ill throughout the day as to be fit for nothing,
but I slept well that night, and about eight in the morning, SUN-
DAY the 29th, came safe to Dublin quay.[2]

LIII

6–21 AUGUST 1790

Ross · Monmouth · Abergavenny · Brecon · Llandovery
Llandeilo · Carmarthen · Llwyn-gwair · Trecwn
Haverfordwest · Roch · Haverfordwest · Pembroke · St. Daniel's
Haverfordwest · Tavernspite · Carmarthen · Llanelli · Swansea
Neath · Pyle · Cowbridge · Llandaf · Cardiff · Newport
Passage · Bristol

[It is doubly unfortunate that there is a gap in the Journal from 4 July to 27
August 1790, for in addition to Wesley's usual comments on persons and places,
his account would have enabled us to compare his first and his last visits to
Wales. Indeed, but for the Diary, we would not know of this visit at all. He
undertook it at the age of 87.]

FRIDAY, 6 AUGUST, 1790

4, [At Bristol] Prayed, tea; 5, chaise; 8, Ross, tea; 9, chaise;
11.15, Monmou[th], at brother Jo[hnson's], writ Journal; 1.15,

---

[1] Not *Claremont*, as in Curnock (viii. 481). *W.H.S. Proc.* v. 75–8.
[2] After a voyage lasting about thirty hours.

dinner, conversed, writ Journal; 4, conversed, visited; 5, tea, conversed; 6, 1 Sam. xxi, 8, visited; 8, supper, conversed, prayer; 9.30.

SATURDAY, 7

4, Prayed, tea, prayer; 5, chaise, Fuller; 8.15, Abergav[enny], tea; 9.30, chaise; 1, Brecon, at brother Church's, writ Journal; 2, dinner, conversed, walk; 3.30, writ Journal, prayed, tea, conversed; 6, 2 Kings ix, 32; visited, prayer, supper, conversed, prayer, on business; 9.30.

SUNDAY, 8

4.30, Prayed, Journal; 7, tea, conversed, Rev. ii, 4! Journal; 11, prayers; 12.30, Mag.; 1, dinner, conversed; 3, sleep, Mag.; 4, prayed, tea, conversed; 6, Lu. xix, 42!, society!, supper, conversed, prayer; 9.45.

MONDAY, 9

3, chaise; 5, at brother Will's,[1] tea, prayer; 6.15, chaise; 8.30, Llandovery; 9.45, chaise; 12, Llandeilo, dinner; 1.30, chaise; 4, Carmarthen; 5, tea, prayed; 6, Isa. lv, 7!, conversed, prayed, supper, conversed, prayer; 9.30.

TUESDAY, 10

4, Prayed, tea; 5, chaise; 10, tea, within; 11, chaise; 1.30, Llwyngwair, writ Journal; 2.30, dinner, conversed, letters; tea, chaise with Mrs. B[owe]n;[2] 6, prayers, Prov. iii, 17!; 7.30, chaise, prayer, supper, conversed; 10.

WEDNESDAY, 11

4.30, Prayed, letters, conversed; 6.30, prayer, tea, conversed; 7.15, chaise, Irish; 11, Trecwn, conversed, Col. iii, 1–4!; 1, dinner, conversed; 2, chaise; 4.30, Haverfordwest, [——] within; 5, tea, conversed; 6, 1 Kings xix, 13, within; 8, supper, conversed; 9.15.

[1] Walter Williams, Beilie (*ante*, p. 104, n. 1.)
[2] Hester Bowen, Llwyn-gwair.

THURSDAY, 12

5, Prayed, letters; 8, tea, conversed, prayer; 9, Mag.; 9.30, chaise with K.W.,[1] *conversed; 11, Roch, Heb. vi, 1!, society, chaise; 1.30, Hav[erfor]d[west], Mag.; 2, dinner, conversed, sleep; 4, prayed; 5, tea, conversed; 6, 1 Pet. i, 24!, society, supper, conversed, prayer; 9.30.*

FRIDAY, 13

4, Prayed, sleep; 6, letters, Journal; 8, tea, conversed, Mag.; 12, walk; 1, dinner, conversed; 2.30, sleep; 3, letter; 5, prayed, conversed; 6, 2 Kings v, 12!, the bands,[2] *supper, within, prayer; 9.15.*

SATURDAY, 14

4, Drest, sleep, letter, Mag.; 8, tea, conversed, Mag.; 10, chaise; 1.15, Pembroke, dinner, conversed; 2.15, sleep, Mag., tea, conversed; 6.30, 1 Sam. xxi, 8!, supper, conversed, prayer; 9.30.

SUNDAY, 15

5, Prayed, letters; 8, tea, conversed, letter, chaise; 10, St. Daniel's, prayer, Acts xi, 36!, meditated; 11, Row [—], communion; 12.30, writ narrative, dinner; 3 [—], boat, chaise, Hav[erfor]d[west]; 5, tea; 5.30, read, Mark i, 15!, the bands, visited, supper, prayer; 9.15.

MONDAY, 16

4, Tea, conversed, prayer; 5, chaise; 8.30, Tavernsp[ite], tea; 9.30, chaise, prayed; 12.30, Carm[arthen]; 1, at T. Taylor's,[3] *writ narrative, dinner, the preachers,*[4] *letters; 4, Isai. xxxv, 8!, on business; 7.30, supper, conversed, prayer; 9.30, lay down; 11.30, sleep.*

---

[1] Kitty Warren.

[2] i.e. the smaller units which, *in toto*, constituted the society.

[3] Thomas Taylor. His wife, who died on 11 Feb. 1825, was a member of the Carmarthen society for over 40 years. *Wes. Meth. Mag.*, 1825, 285.

[4] The Preachers on the Pembrokeshire Circuit were John M'Kersey and James Hall. On 13 Aug. Wesley summoned Thomas Roberts from Bristol to take charge of the Circuit because the previous Assistant (or Superintendent) had 'vilely neglected' it. *Wes. Meth. Mag.*, 1837, 11.

TUESDAY, 17

5.30, Prayed, writ narrative, tea; 7, chaise; 10.30, Llanelli,[1]
*writ narrative; 12, Eph. ii, 8, dinner, conversed; 1.45, chaise
[cipher] ṅ; 4.30, Swans[ea], tea, within, prayed; 6.30, 1 Cor. i,
21, within; 8, supper, conversed, prayer; 9.30.*

WEDNESDAY, 18

*4.30, Prayed, Mag.; 8, tea, conversed; 9, Mag., Journal; 12.30,
chaise; 1.30, H[—]ll house, dinner, conversed; 3.30, chaise; 4.15,
Swansea, prayed, tea; 6, Job. xxii, 21, society; 8, supper, conversed, prayer; 9.30.*

THURSDAY, 19

*4, Prayed, tea, conversed; 5, chaise; 6.30, Neath, tea, conversed;
7.30, Psalm xxxv, 1, chaise; 11, Pyle; 12, chaise; 2, Cowbridge,
at Mr. S[——]ton's;*[2] *dinner, conversed; 3.30, sleep, letter, prayed,
tea, conversed; 6, Matt. xi, 28; 7.30, chaise, Llandaf,*[3] *supper,
conversed; 9, prayer; 9.30.*

FRIDAY, 20

*5, Prayed, letters; 8, tea, conversed, letter; 10, Acts xviii, 17,
dinner; 2, chaise; 4, Llandaf, tea, within; 5.15, chaise, Cardiff;
6, Mark iii, 4!, within, supper, conversed, prayer; 9.30.*

SATURDAY, 21

*4, On business, tea; 5, chaise; 7.30, Newport, tea, conversed; 8.30,
chaise, Irish; 11.30, Passage, small boat; 12, T. Roberts, H. Moore;
12.30, dinner, within; 2, chaise with S. Roberts; 4, Bristol, writ
narrative; 5, prayer; 7, on business; 7.30, Pen[ry]; 8, at Mr.
Castleman's, supper, prayer; 9.30.*

---

[1] On this visit Wesley blessed Henry Child and his wife and gave them a guinea
towards the new preaching-house they intended to build. *Wes. Meth. Mag.*, 1835, 138-9.

[2] A misprint for 'Mrs. Paynton'? On 14 Aug. Wesley had informed Sarah Baker
that he intended calling upon Mrs. Paynton instead of dining with Mr. Flaxman (?)
as he had originally intended. Telford, *Letters*, viii. 233.

[3] Llandaf Court, the home of Thomas Mathews.

APPENDIX 1

John Wesley's Journeys in Wales: an Analysis

No.	Year	Length of visit	Type*
1	1739	15–20 October	A
2	1740	7–12 April	A
3	1741	1–7 October	A
4	1741	15–21 October	A
5	1742	1–6 March	A
6	1742	5–7 July	A
7	1743	3–9 May	A
8	1743	26 September–3 October	A
9	1744	19–28 April	A
10	1745	19–25 July	A
11	1746	11–23 August	A
12	1747	4–8 August	B
13	1747	26 August–5 September	B
14	1748	16 February–8 March	B
15	1748	19–25 May	B
16	1749	17–22 February	A
17	1749	3–15 April	A
18	1750	19 March–7 April	B
19	1753	27–31 August	A
20	1756	18–29 March	B
21	1756	12–14 August	B
22	1758	9–11 August	B
23	1758	21 August–2 September	A
24	1759	2 May	A
25	1760	25 March	A
26	1761	3 April	A
27	1762	29 March	A
28	1763	17–31 August	A
29	1764	25 July–4 August	A

No.	Year	Length of visit	Type*
30	1767	29 August–12 September	A
31	1768	1–13 August	A
32	1769	25–7 July	B
33	1769	9–26 August	A
34	1771	12–31 August	A
35	1772	12–29 August	A
36	1744	15–27 August	A
37	1775	16–28 August	A
38	1777	9–28 July	A
39	1777	29 September–2 October	B
40	1777	14–16 October	B
41	1779	12–28 August	A
42	1781	14–15 April	B
43	1781	23 April–15 May	A
44	1781	December	A
45	1783	10–11 April	B
46	1783	8–9 May	B
47	1784	9–28 August	A
48	1785	8–10 April	B
49	1785	11–13 July	B
50	1787	4 April	B
51	1788	15–30 August	A
52	1789	26–8 March	B
53	1790	6–21 August	A

* *Type (or nature) of Journey:*

A: A specific visit to Wales.
B: A journey through Wales in order to reach another destination.

An Analysis of the Journeys

Type A: John Wesley made thirty-five specific visits to Wales with no other destination in view:

1739–46   Eleven visits were made during these years, and all were made to Monmouthshire, Glamorgan, and Breconshire (Nos. 1–11).

1747–62   Between the Bristol Association of January 1747 and 1762 only eight visits were made to Wales:

2 were made to Garth in Breconshire, the first to arrange the preliminaries of Charles Wesley's marriage and the second to celebrate it (Nos. 16 and 17).

1 was made to Chepstow, possibly to open the New Room there (No. 27).

3 were made to Mold, Flintshire (Nos. 24, 25, and 26).

2 (and only 2) were made to Glamorgan, the one (No. 19) to resuscitate the society at Cardiff, the other (No. 23) to fulfil a promise made earlier in the month.

1763–90   15 visits were made during these years to south-west (as well as south-east) Wales (Nos. 28, 29, 30, 31, 33, 34, 35, 36, 37, 38, 41, 43, 47, 51, 53).

1 visit was made to Wrexham (No. 44).

Type B: In addition to these specific visits to Wales, John Wesley passed through the country on eighteen other occasions to or from Ireland:

1. Nine of these journeys were made to Ireland:

(*a*) 4 were made through South and Central Wales to Holyhead (Nos. 12, 14, 18, 20).

(*b*) 4 were made through North Wales from Chester to Holyhead (Nos. 45, 48, 50, 52).

(*c*) 1 was (probably) made through South Wales to Fishguard (No. 39).

2. Nine others were made from Ireland:

(*a*) 6 were made from Holyhead to Chester through North Wales. (Nos. 21, 32, 40, 42, 46, 49).

(*b*) 2 were made from Holyhead through Central and South Wales to Bristol (Nos. 13, 15).

(*c*) 1 was made by sea from Dublin to Pen-clawdd (No. 22).

3. On only six occasions however did Wesley make the outward and inward journey through Wales, as the following table shows:

To Ireland:	12	14	18	20	*	*	39	*	45	48	50	52
From Ireland:	13	15	*	21	22	32	40	42	46	49	*	*

He sailed to Ireland from Liverpool in 1758 and 1781 and from Parkgate in 1769 (the outward journeys corresponding to return journeys Nos. 22, 42, and 32 respectively); and he returned to Bristol from Dublin in 1750 and to Parkgate in 1787 and 1789 (after making the outward journeys Nos. 18, 50, and 52).

APPENDIX 2

A. Persons referred to in the Journal

A[llgoo]d (?), Mrs.

B., Mr.
Baker, Sarah.
Bissicks, Thomas.
Bowen, George.
Bowen, Hester.
Bradford, Joseph.
Broadbent, John.

C[atchmay(d)], Mr.
Cheek, Moseley.
Colley, Wilfred.
Cook, Lieutenant.

Davies, the Revd. Howell.
Davies, the Revd. Thomas.
Deer, John.
Deer, Sister.

Ellis, the Revd. Thomas.
E[van]s, the Revd. Mr.
Evans, the Revd. William (?).

Fletcher, the Revd. John.

Glascott, Thomas.
Goodwin, Mr.
Griffith, William.
Griffiths, Robert.
G[winnett] (?), Mr.
Gwynne, Howell (?).
Gwynne, Marmaduke (sen.).
Gwynne, Marmaduke (jun.) (?).
Gwynne, Sarah.

Harris, Howell.
Haswell, Jane.
Haughton, John.
Hodges, the Revd. John.
Holloway, [Walter ?].
Hopper, Christopher.
Humphreys, Joseph.

Huntingdon, Selina Countess of.

Jaco, Peter.
James, Mrs. Elizabeth.
James, Thomas (?)
James, the Revd. William.
Jane, John.
Jenkins, Ann.
Johnson, [Thomas ?].
Jones, Mary.
Jones, Robert.
Jones, Robert (jun.).
Jones, William.

Lewis, John.
Lloyd, Henry.

Mansel, Bussy, 4th Baron.
Mathews, Thomas.
Morgan, James.
Morgan, Jenkin.
Morgan, Mrs.
Morris, Valentine.

Newell, Nancy.
Newton, the Revd. John.

P., Sir T.
Perronet, Charles.
Phillips, the Revd. Edward.
Price, Arthur.
Price, John.
Price, Thomas.
Prichard, William.
Prickard, John.
Prosser, Thomas.
Protheroe, Marmaduke (?).
Pugh, the Revd. David.

Rees, the Revd. William (?).
Reeves, Jonathan.
Rice, George.
Roberts, William.

Rowland, the Revd. Daniel.

St. Leger, Col. [Barry].
Stepney, Sir Thomas.
S[tokes, John Rees ?], Mr.
Story, George.
Swindells, Robert.

Talbot, the Revd. Thomas.
Thomas, Howell.
Thomas, Thomas.
Tucker, William.
Turner, Capt. Joseph.

Vaughan, Admiral.

Walsh, the Revd. Thomas.
Warren, Miss Catherine.
W[aters], Mr.
W[ells, the Revd. Nathaniel ?].
Wesley, the Revd. Charles.
Whitefield, the Revd. George.
Williams, [Nathaniel ?].
Williams, the Revd. Peter.
Williams, Thomas.
Williams, the Revd. William.

B. *Places referred to in the Journal*

Aberdare
Abergavenny
Aberthaw
Aberystwyth

Bangor
Bedwas
Bonvilston
Brecon
Bridgend
Builth

Caerleon
Caernarfon
Caerphilly
Caldicot
Cardiff
Cardigan
Carmarthen
Chepstow
Clyro
Conway
Cowbridge
Coychurch
Crickhowell

Dale
Devauden
Dinas Mawddwy
Dolgellau

Fishguard
Fonmon
Fountain Head inn, The
Ffair-rhos
Ffontygari

Garth
Gelli-gaer
Glan-y-gors
Gwindy

Haverfordwest
Hay
Holyhead
Holywell
Houghton

Jeffreston

Kidwelly
Kinmel

Lampeter
Lamphey
Laugharne
Little Newcasıle
Loughor ferry
Llanbradach
Llandaf
Llandeilo
Llanddaniel-fab
Llan-ddew
Llanelli
Llanfaches
Llanfihangel Tre'r-beirdd
Llangefni
Llanhilleth
Llanidloes
Llanishen
Llan-maes
Llanmartin
Llannerch-y-medd

C. *Persons and places referred to in the Diary only*

Map 1. Some routes followed by John Wesley.

KEY:

LLANIDLOES – Places referred to in the Journal or Diary.

The Ferries:

1. Old Passage
2. New Passage
3. Ferry across R. Neath
4. Ferry across R. Tawe
5. Loughor
6. Llanstephan
7. Laugharne
8. Pembroke to Burton
9. Conway
10. Talycafn
11. Bangor
12. Porthaethwy
13. Moel y don

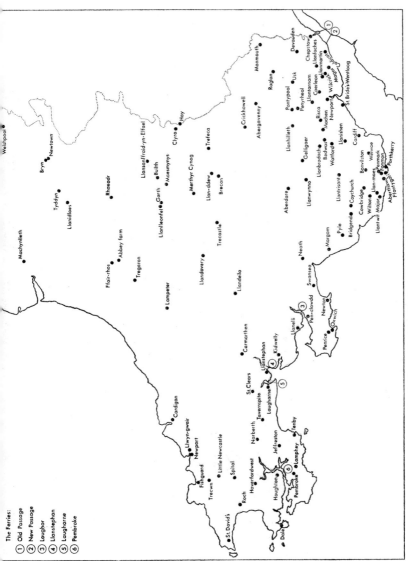

The Ferries:
① Old Passage
② New Passage
③ Loughor
④ Llanstephan
⑤ Loughorne
⑥ Pembroke

Map 2. Places visited by John Wesley in South and Central Wales.

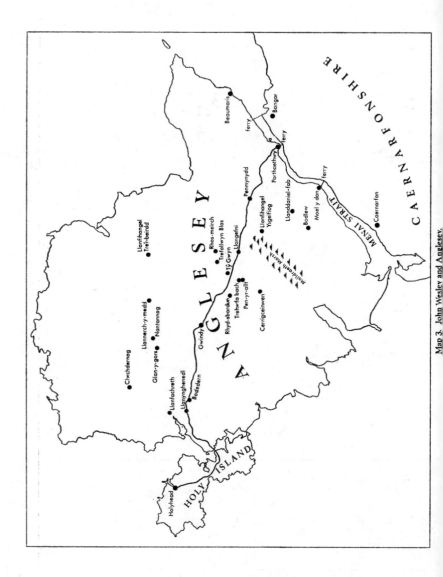

Map 3. John Wesley and Anglesey.

INDEX

PRINTED IN GREAT BRITAIN
AT THE UNIVERSITY PRESS, OXFORD
BY VIVIAN RIDLER
PRINTER TO THE UNIVERSITY